Design Your Dream Life

The Young Adult's Guide to Building Your Life Using Money

Answers on How to Save, Invest, Think About Money and More!

Urenna Chimso

Published by Izuchi LLC

First paperback edition August 2022

Artwork provided through Canva
Edited by Gracie Rose

ISBN 979-8-9868126-0-1 (paperback)
ISBN 979-8-9868126-1-8 (kindle)

*Providing people
with knowledge to
share in my
confidence to
design the lives we
desire.*

Contents

Preface

Clueless is the word that describes most of our relationships with money. Considering that money is part of every aspect of our lives, it's important to know how to use it to our advantage, and yet we're raised with little to no education on the matter. Our first big financial decisions — buying a car and going to college — usually put us in debt. In fact, a lot of financial advertising is geared towards getting us to borrow instead of to own. We see wealthy people and think such a life is only attainable by having rich parents or by being in the unconscious state that is dreaming. I was also clueless when it came to money. I got sucked into a pyramid scheme and lost hundreds of dollars in the meme currency, Dogecoin. Thanks to the guidance of my parents, I was able to educate myself on money. I'm now using that knowledge to construct the life of my dreams. Here's a little bit of my story.

I was raised with a basic understanding of financial literacy. My dad put me and my brothers on a budget when I was 13; my mom had us work at her business during breaks and pay for things we wanted; I saw my mom give talks at conferences about taxes and real estate. When I started working full-time summers at 15, I quickly realized that this whole work thing was not for me. My only real ambitions in life were to have a family and not work. I wanted to learn how I could retire as early as possible. The summer after I turned 18, my mom gave me some money to invest in the stock market. I had no idea what to do except let it sit for a little while to grow. But, how long was "a little while?"

In my pursuit of learning how to retire early, I realized that I grew up with more financial literacy than most people. I developed a passion for educating other people — especially young people — about money but as I tried to educate others, I quickly realized how much I actually didn't know. All I knew to do was budget, save, work, and stay out of debt but knew absolutely nothing about investing, credit, or taxes. As I tried to become financially literate, I became more and more discouraged because the minute I learned something, I realized there were about ten other things that I didn't know I didn't know; you know the saying "you don't know what you don't know." Online information about finances is very scattered and full of people's opinions and get-rich-quick schemes, which I fell prey to. The summer before my sophomore year of college, I became a licensed investment advisor, per the advice of my dad, and my cluelessness disappeared.

At the end of my sophomore year, my dad presented the idea of writing a book on personal finance to share the knowledge I had gained from the previous summer. This book is designed as an accessible resource on personal finance. The Q&A nature of it makes it a very easy read and allows you to pick it up and drop it whenever you please. If today you're curious about budgeting, just read the budgeting questions and go about your day. If you need some really quick information on real estate before you start looking for properties, just flip to the back of the book and find what you're looking for. You can get exactly the information you're looking for without the fluff; however, there is fluff at the beginning of each section if that is something you enjoy.

My goal for writing this book was to create a resource that makes talking and learning about money easier and more accessible to the average person. I provide both information about different areas of finances and the practical advice you need to take control of your money today. I teach you how you can employ your money and not just be employed for money. The information in this book is meant to teach you how to use money not only to sustain you but to make you thrive. I know not everyone has people to guide them through finances like I did, but let this book be the guidance, education, and catalyst for your financial development. I hope that each time you pick up this book — whether for a quick question, some advice and inspiration, or for an entire read through — you drop it having gained knowledge, confidence, a plan, and a vision to design and create the life of your dreams.

Mindset

Laying the Foundation

Uche is a 28-year-old architect living in New York. He currently has a Mercedes, always has the newest iPhone, and only wears customly designed sneakers. He's always buying expensive gifts for his girlfriend and always suggests high-end restaurants to eat out with his friends. Throughout grade school, he was nicknamed "Nuke" because, in the fifth grade, he wore a pair of knock-off Nike sneakers. Since then, his primary goal has been to become rich so no one could embarrass him again. In the pursuit of being rich, he makes most of his purchases on credit cards, going into debt to keep up his appearance. Everyone around him thinks he's balling, and he thinks that being rich is what he's made to be, but he doesn't realize that he does all this to cater to the self-esteem of the 10-year old boy who was embarrassed for wearing knock-off shoes.

When you think about getting your money in order, what comes to mind? Spending less? Creating a budget? Maybe investing? While those things are important and will be covered later in this book, the real driving force behind money in our lives is our mindset towards it. The way we think about money affects what we do with it, and what we do with our money has a massive effect on our lives.

Almost everyone has the basic mindset of getting and spending money, but each of us have our own personal ideas that affect how we do those two things. Some of us are scared of spending money on anything because we feel we never have enough. Some of us spend everything as a coping mechanism. Some of us think money is the root of all evil, and some of us think it's the answer to all of our problems. These underlying ideas create defaults in our relationship with money, and not being aware of them can have consequences.

I put "Mindset" as the first part of this book because having a healthy view of money is the key to transforming your finances. Until Uche is able to address what happened in the fifth grade, he'll continue to make financial decisions from that place of hurt. The questions and answers in this section — and throughout the rest of the book — are here to help you form a healthy view of money so you can control it for your benefit and flourish. As you read, examine your internal thoughts about money, where they came from, how they affect your relationship with money, and — if need be — how you can replace them with more empowering views.

What is the purpose of money?
Money exists so that we can efficiently exchange goods and services with other members in our economy. In our personal lives, money's purpose is to give us the ability to get the things, services, and experiences we want. The purpose of money is not to simply have it or show it off. The question then becomes, how do I get the money to accomplish the things I want and need?

Why can't we just get rid of money? It causes so many problems in the world.
Let's look at the history and evolution of money. To start, money only exists because humans are communal, intelligent beings with different abilities but the same basic needs. We need food, shelter, water, and safety to survive. Humans went from being self-sufficient within their individual

families to being self-sufficient within tribes and groups. Within that self-sufficiency, roles were assigned to meet the different needs: men hunted and protected; women cultivated and maintained. As populations grew, it became harder to remain purely communal. Tribes would either divide into smaller tribes or move towards barter, the exchange of one good for another. Barter is relatively efficient in terms of exchange but not efficient in terms determining the value of a good. The efficiency of standardized valuation led to the development of money.

The history continued as money advanced from shells to paper and now to cryptocurrency but the essence remained the same from that point on. Money exists as the most efficient way to exchange goods and services within an ever-growing society, economy, and world to meet the needs and desires of individuals, families, and nations. If we were to somehow rid the world of all traces of money, we would find ourselves right back in the same position generations down the line. The thing we should be thinking about is how to minimize the problems money causes instead of trying to get rid of it.

"A life with financial wealth but no relational, emotional, mental, spiritual, and physical wealth is an empty life."

Is money really that important?
Considering that everything we do and need is based on the exchange of goods and services and our mode of exchange is money, yes, money is really that important. Unless you're going to be doing everything from scratch, you need money. Even just looking at our most basic needs — food, water, shelter, and maybe clothing — you still need to buy materials to garden, build your own house, make your own clothes, and, if you want clean water, you're most likely going to buy a filtration system for the water you collect. At this stage of human development, you basically need money to live.

What are the most important areas financially?

There are numerous areas to consider but these are the main ones from which all other categories stem from:

Financial Tree of Life

- MONEY!!!
- Stocks
- Real Estate
- Income/Budget
- Net Worth
- Bonds
- Mindset/Habits
- Vision/Goals
- Financial Literacy
- Network/Circle

- ❖ Financial Literacy
- ❖ Goals and Vision
- ❖ Mindset and Habits
- ❖ Income and Budget
- ❖ Network and Circle
- ❖ Net Worth

You might've been expecting me to say stocks, a retirement account, taxes, insurance, and a bunch of other explicitly financial areas. While these areas are essential in the consideration of your financial life, they are not the basis on which it stands. Think of the first five areas as the roots of your financial life and the sixth as its trunk. Trees grow from the roots up, and if the roots are suffering, the rest of the tree suffers. Your net worth is the trunk because it's a result of the strength of the first five areas, the roots. The branches — the explicit financial areas — protrude from the trunk and create leaves — money. Whoever said money doesn't grow on trees clearly didn't know what they were talking about. Below is my personal story of how this analogy plays out but I want to expand a bit on your network and circle since there's no section for them in the book

There are two sayings that sum up the importance of who's around you: "You're the average of the five people you spend the most time with": "Your network = your net worth". The people we surround ourselves with have great impacts on our lives, in ways we are both aware and unaware of. If you want to grow financially, connect with people who have similar goals, who have done what you're trying to do, and even people who you can influence to do the same. You don't always need to talk about money but having their influence in your life will cause your goals, mindset, and habits around money to evolve.

When I turned 18, I developed this vision that I want to retire in my 30s (vision), at 35 specifically (goal), because I don't enjoy working (mindset). The extent of my financial literacy at that point was knowing that work and budgets are essential, having debt is bad, and that somehow people can get rich from stocks (literacy and mindset). I had developed a habit of budgeting and not spending money since I was 13 years old (habit, budget) and worked for my mom during breaks to earn money (income).

Not long after my 18th birthday, my mom gave me some money to invest in the stock market and took me to get a credit card (net worth). The problem was, I had absolutely no idea what to do with either of those things (literacy) and felt like I had no one to talk to and help me with my vision (circle). Fast forward to the summer after I turned 19, I became a licensed investment adviser and had an abundance of financial knowledge (literacy). The problem this time was that almost all the money I was earning was used to pay for school (income). Because I felt like I had no money (mindset), I lost the habit of budgeting and spent all of the little money I did have instead of budgeting and investing some of it (habit).

I knew that I wanted to invest in real estate to earn passive income for early retirement (literacy and goal) but didn't know where to start (literacy) and didn't think it was possible for a 19 year old to own property (mindset, circle). During my sophomore year of college, I was encouraged by one of my friends who, at 21, bought a property (circle). When I went home for the summer, I started talking to my parents more about my goal (goal, network) and was able to buy a rental property to increase my assets and passive income (net worth). That year, I also started budgeting (budget) my leftover money and making contributions to my investment account (habit, net worth). Now, I manage a rental property and contribute to my investments to build my assets and income (habit) for early retirement (goal). I'm hoping I can find more people my age who are on the same journey so we can encourage and help each other reach our goals (network).

I encourage you to be mindful and always actively work on the five roots of your financial life. They not only affect your net worth and the progress of your goals, but they also affect each other and have compounding impacts on the health of your financial life.

What is wealth?

Wealth — in the financial sense — is the possession of an abundance of valuable assets, whether financial or physical, that can be converted into money. Although wealth is always conflated with money, money is not the only factor in holistic wealth. Holistic wealth is the well-being of your finances, emotions, relationships, mind, spirit, and physical body. A life with financial wealth but no relational, emotional, mental, spiritual, and physical wealth is an empty life. Never let your holistic wealth fall by the wayside in pursuit of financial wealth.

What is an asset?

An asset is something of quality that is useful. People can be assets, abilities can be assets, possessions can be assets, ideas can be assets, etc. A financial asset is something that you own that has monetary value and/or has the potential to increase in value. Financial assets include things like stocks, bonds, real estate, businesses, boats, and expensive jewelry. Assets are primarily used in the interest of building wealth.

"Strive to be wealthy, not to look rich"

What is a liability?

A liability is something that diminishes the value and quality of something else. A bad employee, bad behavior, and negative perception can all be liabilities. A financial liability is money owed back to someone else, or debt. Liabilities can come in the form of a leased car, an unpaid home, a credit card, or student loans. Liabilities are primarily acquired to get something you don't currently have the money to pay for, and they can diminish the value of your wealth.

What is net worth?

Net Worth = Assets - Liabilities; what is owned minus what is owed. Net worth is the way in which your wealth is measured; the higher your net worth, the wealthier you are. This number is not about how much money you get but how much you're able to keep. Someone who earns $50k a year could have a net worth of $1 million while someone who earns $150k a year has a net worth of $500k because they keep more of their money rather than spending or borrowing. The earlier you start to build your net worth, the higher it will be in the long run.

Are being rich and wealthy the same thing?

Yes and no. They do have the same definition but the understanding of them is different. Someone can be rich and not wealthy, someone can be wealthy but not appear rich, and someone can both be wealthy and appear rich. The idea of being rich is all in perception: wearing designer brands; driving an expensive car; having a big house; going on many exotic vacations; etc. To do these things you do need a lot of money, but that doesn't mean that the money used is your money. Many people are in severe debt all in the name of appearing rich. As mentioned above, being wealthy is having a lot of valuable assets that provide you with significant amounts of money. A wealthy person can have 20 paid-off rental properties but live in a townhome and drive a Toyota. They can have a self-running business and live in an apartment with no car because they are constantly traveling. They can have $2 million in the stock market and three kids who all go to public school and wear H&M clothes. It's more important to strive to be wealthy rather than looking rich.

What is financial literacy?

Financial literacy is having the knowledge about how money operates within our society and the world as a whole to make informed, educated, and effective decisions regarding money for various goals.

Why is financial literacy important?

Financial literacy is important because almost everything we do involves money in some shape or form, and the only way most people know how to get money is by working for it. Financial literacy gives you the knowledge you need to make money work for you, and — as a result — work for it less. By being financially literate you can introduce more time, flexibility, control and peace into your life.

You can always make more money. Why do I need to learn about financial literacy if I can always make back what I spend?

Financial literacy is not just about knowing how to make money but about knowing how to effectively use your money so you don't always have to chase after it. It is true, to a certain extent, that you can always make back the money that you spend, but that mindset keeps you in a cycle of constantly working for money instead of having the mindset that your money can work for you. Once you switch your mindset, you start thinking of ways in which you can "employ" your money, and the process of discovering those ways is through financial literacy.

What are good questions to ask to become more financially literate?

A good general question to ask is "How does this work?" You can apply this to stocks, bonds, budgeting, investing, income, real estate and honestly anything else. Knowing how something works is the foundation to true understanding and enables you to ask more specific questions that will drive your education. Here are a list of other good questions you can research:

- What are different ways I can make income?
- What is passive income?
- How can I make passive income?
- What are different investment avenues?
- What's the best use of my money?
- Why does everything cost money?
- What steps can I take toward retirement?
- How can I retire early?
- Who do I have around me that knows a lot about money?

Where do I go to start learning about money? What are some good resources to learn more about finances?

Khan Academy has a free Personal Finance course that offers advice and education on everything from budgeting to buying a house to saving for retirement. Just like all other content on the platform, the Personal Finance lessons come in video form with multiple videos for each topic and subtopic.

NerdWallet is a website that offers beginner-friendly financial education, calculators, and comparisons of popular financial products. Through their website, you can learn about different index funds, calculate how much you would need to invest for retirement, and choose a broker to help you execute your investment goals.

The Balance is a website that offers beginner-friendly financial and economic education and calculators for mortgages and budgeting. They provide very practical tips to manage your finances, from creating a financial plan to managing a mortgage.

Investopedia is a website that offers education on equity investments and the economy and provides rankings for various financial service providers. Someone who already has a basic understanding of investments and the economy would benefit from their information because they explain principles in depth.

The Motley Fool is very similar to Investopedia in that they provide education and rankings on equity investments but they also provide information on loans (credit cards, mortgages, and bank loans). Additionally, they provide a bit more beginner-friendly advice and information in their "101" articles.

What is financial freedom?

Financial freedom is the state where your assets are producing enough passive income to completely replace your earned income. At this point, you can choose whether or not to continue working, but your work is no longer motivated by the need to sustain your life, and you are now financially free from the reality of working to live.

"Your goals are shaped around what is important to you"

Is financial freedom really as simple as knowing everything you need to do?

Having the knowledge, which is financial literacy, is only one of the roots of your financial life. Like I said previously, all the roots interact with and affect each other. You can know about investing but if you don't have a habit of being disciplined with your budget, you won't make any progress. You may know that real estate is a great way to earn passive income but if you don't have people to help you develop a buying strategy, you could waste five years before you actually buy a property. If you know exactly where you want to be in five years and how to get there but don't have a job, you will make no progress. Your financial life is holistic and requires maintaining all roots for it to be successful.

What things should I consider as I'm going on my financial journey?
As mentioned earlier, a vision of what you want your life to look like will fuel the decisions you make around your finances, so having that established will dictate most of the decisions you make. Some practical things to consider on your financial journey are planning for retirement, owning property (as a homeowner or an investor), your spending habits, protecting your assets, having kids, and passing on your assets.

How do I set financial goals?
As you're setting financial goals, it's important to remember that your finances exist to help you accomplish the things you want and need in life. Your goals are shaped around what is important to you. A good starting place is writing down your values and the ways in which money can help you live out those values. Below is an outline of how you can go about setting and accomplishing your financial goals.

1. Evaluate your visions, needs, and wants
2. Set material or monetary goals around your vision
3. Determine the money needed to achieve each goal
4. Establish a time frame for each goal
5. Choose investment strategies to accomplish each goal in time
6. Set short-term and long-term investing and savings goals
7. Have income streams and a budget that incorporate your money goals and your current needs and wants
8. Be disciplined and consistent with your budget
9. Have backup plans and be flexible

It's really hard for me to see myself in a better financial state. What do you suggest I do to change my mindset? How do I practically achieve my financial goals?
The most important thing is to prove yourself wrong, no matter how small your progress is. Being better just means that you've improved from where you were before. If you don't have a budget, start by creating one; this is

the defining step to improving your finances. If you don't have a safety net, start saving for one; you'll be better with one. If you don't have any investments, put $10 into an index fund today. It's better than $0. The little things we do everyday make the big differences in our life. Once you start seeing that it's not hard to be in a better place, you'll start believing more in your ability to achieve your financial goals

Another thing to do is address why it's hard for you to see yourself in a better state. A lot of our financial mindsets come from how we were raised. Ask yourself a few questions to get to the root of that disbelief: How did my parents talk about money?; How did I view money growing up? Was money a thing we had growing up or something we were always trying to get?; Does my financial state now reflect the financial state I grew up in? Once you answer these questions, you'll have a better understanding of what's really causing you to have unbelief and be able to assess whether that basis is still relevant in your life.

What if my parents never taught me about money?
It's never too late to take control of your education and your money. Actually, most people grow up not being taught about financial literacy and have their first real encounters with finances when they graduate college. If your parents didn't teach you about money growing up, you're not alone. Something my mom always says is "adults parent themselves". As an adult, your education and money are now your responsibilities. Reading this book is a huge step in the right direction because you will learn more than enough to start your journey to a healthy financial life. Continue to educate yourself and implement the things you learn.

What does it take to become wealthy?
It takes a lot of discipline, a lot of consistency, patience, and a strategy. Wealth is all about building and accumulating assets, and the road to get there is filled with many practical, day-to-day habits within and outside your financial life. All the roots of your financial life will determine where

you end up in your wealth journey so it's important to be mindful of each of them, especially your mindset and habits. In terms of material things, stock, investments, and real estate are the essential ways in which people build their wealth.

What are some lies that affect young people's relationship with money?
Everyone has preconceptions about money — some good, some bad — based on their background and experiences. The key thing to consider as you reflect on your own thoughts is whether or not that thought positively contributes to your financial goals. If it doesn't, understand where that idea came from and replace that thought with the truth. Here are a few examples of bad preconceptions young people may have.

- ❖ I have time before I need to really start worrying about my finances
- ❖ These are "the best years of my life," and I need to enjoy them as much as I can
- ❖ If I want it and can afford it, I should buy it
- ❖ I need a lot of money to start investing
- ❖ I'll be responsible when I'm married and have a family
- ❖ Credit cards are for emergencies
- ❖ I need OPM (other people's money) to build wealth

What do I do when I'm trying to get my finances together but my friends always want to do activities that cost money?
Be honest about where you're at and the journey you're on. They may not know you're trying to cut back on spending, and telling them may encourage them to start thinking of their own financial journeys. You can also propose activities that are free or low-cost like movie and game nights, going to a park, walking or biking around the city, having picnics, going on a hike or to a lake, and so many other fun and cheap activities.

How do I manage my emotions with a constantly changing market?
You need to understand your goals and the market. The markets are
constantly changing, but they change more frequently in the short term
and tend to do well in the long run. If your goals are short-term, it's better
to use strategies that are relatively stable during market changes. If your
goals are long-term, you need not worry about short-term market changes,
whether good or bad. In the past 100 years of the economy, we have seen a
growth averaging out to about 8% - 10% a year over a 10-year period, even
with major economic shocks. Having an understanding of this will help you
not to be consumed by the daily shifts of the market.

Who should I listen to about the state of the markets/economy?
Almost everyone has something to say about the economy but a lot of
information out there, whether from the news or from friends, can be
based on opinion, uninformed observation, and speculation. It's best to
listen to historically trusted financial news outlets because they specialize
in economic analysis and projections and have proven accurate and
useful throughout the history of our economy. A few great sources are The
Wall Street Journal, Forbes, The Economist, and Bloomberg. They may
require a subscription to access some of their content but subscribing to
at least one resource is a good investment to stay informed on economic
issues.

*"The little things we do everyday are the things make the big
differences in our life"*

*Should I jump on financial bandwagons? If everyone is doing it, there must
be something there, right?*
Bandwagons are one of the riskiest ways to make financial decisions.
There's widespread financial advice that has been proven effective for
decades and generations. Bandwagons tend to be short-term decisions
that are saturating society, not amongst investors but amongst the

general, oftentimes uneducated, public. They also tend to advertise getting rich quickly and there's always high risk with investments that promise high returns. Financial bandwagons are an after-the-fact way for people to get involved in investments that are surprisingly successful; they join because of their vast growth and assume that the growth will continue. You don't hear widespread talk about good investments while they're still developing; you hear about them once they've boomed. With everyone talking about and investing in them, they often lead to bubbles and subsequently crashes, causing most people to lose the money they invested. This happened with the dot-com bubble in the 90s, with the real estate market in 2007, and even with bitcoin and cryptocurrency in 2021, which I unfortunately got caught up in. There's a saying by Joe Kennedy, JFK's dad, that is common amongst seasoned investors: "If shoe shine boys are giving stock tips, then it's time to get out of the market."

I've seen a lot of people on social media making expensive purchases and reaching their financial goals, and I'm both inspired and intimidated by them. How do I know that my goals are really MY goals and not what I see other people doing?

Remember your goals arise from your vision of your life. Always go back to your vision and ask yourself, "Is this goal aligned with what I ultimately want in my life?" Another great question to ask yourself is "If I didn't see anyone with it, would I still want it?" You can also take some time away from social media to see how those goals persist when you're not constantly seeing what other people are doing. It's not bad if you get inspiration from others' accomplishments or if some of your goals are aligned with those of other people, but just remember that your goals are a reflection of your vision. If it doesn't directly contribute to your vision, or even takes away from it, then it might be a goal that's not genuinely yours.

Conversations about money make me anxious, but I know it's an important aspect of being an adult. How do I deal with my feelings so I can have a healthy relationship with my finances?

You need to identify what exactly it is about money that makes you anxious. If you don't address the root problem, it'll continue to affect you in different ways until you do. It could be the way you were raised, the way your parents talked about money, how you've seen other people use money, or a money mistake you've made that you haven't emotionally dealt with. Even just understanding the root can contribute to you feeling less anxious. Once you've discovered the root problem, you have to be consistent in encouraging yourself every time that thought or feeling comes up because your anxiety can cause you to make irrational decisions with your money or even cause you to be stagnant. It really helps to surround yourself with people who are also trying to improve their finances so they can encourage you as well; they might also have similar feelings and knowing that can help you to feel less anxious.

"Money is a tool, not the goal"

What advice would you give to someone who struggles with retail therapy or spending money impulsively?

This is a matter of addressing your mindset and habits. Impulsive spending, which includes retail therapy, is a reactive coping mechanism to some trigger. You may feel inclined to spend when you feel anxious, when someone has upset you, or during a time of the year that's particularly stressful. It may take a little while to identify your triggers but every time you notice yourself spending impulsively, take time to trace back to the cause. Once you identify your triggers, you need to understand why spending is your way of coping so you can find better ways to cope. A great way to cope is by writing your thoughts down and by talking things out with friends. Your friends should be able to both advise you and hold you accountable with your spending. You're going to need to be honest and transparent with yourself and your friends to see progress.

Our society can be very materialistic and money-focused, and it's very easy to become consumed by this culture. How do I work on my finances without becoming too "money-minded"?
Understand that money is a tool and not the goal; it is a means to an end and not the end itself. I will always say this — your vision and goals are the driving force behind everything related to your finances, whether or not you're aware of them. To avoid becoming too "money-minded," always remind yourself what you're working towards and how the money will help you achieve those dreams. You can also avoid this mentality by enjoying your life now and not only living for the future. You don't want to find that, when you finally achieve your goals, you are not able to live in the present and enjoy what you've been striving for. You're living life now and you will live it in the future, so you might as well enjoy it at any stage that you're in.

How can I work towards financial freedom if I don't have a lot of income?
Focus on developing the roots of your financial life mentioned above. These areas hold true for any situation life throws at you. Specifically, if you don't have a lot of income, I would say to focus heavily on your goals and your income. First, see if there are ways you can increase your income by developing other streams of income or increasing your professional value. As you're doing that, create a budget, if you don't already have one, and focus on being disciplined to stick to it; this will be a habit that will benefit you throughout your entire life. Your income and budget address your current situation; goals and vision address your future. Start envisioning your future and your long-term goals by writing them down and thinking about what your finances need to look like to achieve them. Practically, write down some realistic numbers of where you want your finances to be in the next year and consistently work towards them. You will need to be financially literate to effectively implement this change, so

always have a mindset of learning, and be disciplined. The habits you develop in this stage of your life will sustain you when you start achieving your financial goals.

So I have a fear of spending money and tend to hoard it even when I know there are things I NEED to buy. I do pretty good with saving and investing, but spending my own money makes me anxious. What can I do to break this fear?

First, you need to understand that money is meant to be spent, whether now or in the future. Your fear of spending money is most likely a reaction you've developed from a time in your life where you felt like you didn't have enough money. A way you could address this fear is by having a combined zero-based and envelope budget *(check money management section for more detail)*. With the envelope part, you'll allocate all of your income into different spending categories so you know how much to spend on each thing; make sure you include categories for social activities. If by the end of the month you have some leftover money from some categories, you'll put that money into your savings and investments and repeat for the next month. Making a spending plan can reduce some of the anxiety you feel towards spending your money because you know exactly how much you have and where everything is going. There will be some months where you have money leftover, and seeing that extra money will show you that you actually have more than enough to do everything you need and want to do. It will be hard to let go of the money at first, but, as you keep doing it, you'll notice your anxiety diminish and eventually go away.

Income

Expanding Your Options

Chisom is a 26 year old high school Algebra teacher who is looking for ways she can earn some extra money each month. Currently, she babysits for a few friends whenever they have date nights. She's talked to her sisters about this and found out that one of them does DoorDash on the weekends, one of them does freelance writing here and there, and the other is currently creating an online course about sewing and upcycling. Talking with her sisters got her thinking about her different skills she could possibly monetize. She's thinking about starting a weekly college application coaching session for the kids of her parents' friends.

Now that we have an understanding of the role of money in our lives, it's time to address step one in finances: having some money. For 8 hours a day, 5 days a week, 52 weeks a year, for 40 years of our lives, we get up and go to work to have the time of our lives and to make a difference in the world. Well, that's what I was told at my graduation. The main reason we work is so we can have income to go out, buy gifts, and dress up in really fancy clothes for parties at the same place that gave us the income. Truthfully, the reason we need income is so we can live.

Considering earning income takes up such a large portion of our lives — and it's the basis on which all money decisions are made — it's important to talk about the different ways it can be earned. Since we all know the traditional way of earning income is being employed, I've decided to focus on other ways in which we can earn income. My focus on alternative avenues is not meant to downplay traditional jobs. A traditional job is always a valuable thing to have and the most secure way of earning income. I just want to provide a perspective on more ways you could earn money.

As mentioned in the previous section, your income is one of the roots of your financial life. Without income, you have nothing to apply all of your knowledge to. This section is meant to give you ideas of ways you can make money so you can maximize the base on which you build your wealth.

What is income?
Income is money that is received, usually on a regular basis, for work or through investments. For budgeting purposes, income is any money you receive, whether through work, investments, as a gift, or by inheritance.

Why is life so expensive?
A question every adult constantly asks themselves, and a very valid one at that. We live in a highly specialized, highly efficient, fairly individualistic economy and society. As a result, we don't live self-sufficiently and rely on other people for our basic necessities like food, water, shelter, clothes, and safety. Some of these needs are provided through our government, which we pay for with taxes, but we are responsible for getting everything else. Because we depend on farmers for food, builders for houses, and brands for clothes, we pay them for the services and products we're not providing ourselves. You could very well grow your own food, build your own house, and make your own clothes. However, you would lose time, efficiency, and quality. Efficiency is the main reason why we essentially pay to live and will continue to pay for more things as society develops. If you want to pay less, are you willing to sacrifice the time and energy that comes with being more self-sufficient?

How do I make more money?

Most people make money from their jobs and there are two ways employees are paid: by wage or by salary. If you're a wage worker, you can make more money by either working more hours or jobs or finding a way to increase your wage, inside or outside your current job. For salary workers, you can negotiate with your boss for a raise or find a job that pays you a higher salary. You can also have side hustles that bring in some extra money like doing DoorDash, doing hair, tutoring, or babysitting. For side hustles, try to offer services instead of goods — that way you're directly being paid for the time you put in.

How can I make more money in less time?

The only way to increase the amount of money you earn in a certain period of time is to increase your earnings per period. You could make more money in a week if you picked up an extra shift or an extra job but that answers the "more money" part and not the "less time" part. To earn more money in less time you have to increase your value within the job market, which is often tied to increased skill and ability. You can increase your knowledge, and therefore your skill, with another degree or a certification. You can find ways to improve the company you work at and subsequently negotiate a raise with your employer. You can spend time developing a product that sells itself. The key here is to ask yourself "How can I add more value to myself and to those around me?" You can also decrease your time by selling results and becoming highly efficient at producing those results. Let's say you create websites and charge $600 per site. It takes you about ten hours to create each website, so you're earning $60/hr. By becoming more efficient and cutting that time down to six hours, you increase your earning potential from $60/hr to $100/hr.

Are there easy ways to make money? If so, what are they?

The easiest way to make money is to have streams of passive income but in order to have passive income you need investments and investments require money and time. Outside of passive income, the easiest way to make money is to have a stable job. While it may not feel easy because it takes eight hours of your day, it's a lot easier than trying to work for yourself or build a business. When you're employed, you have a set work schedule and stable income, while neither is guaranteed when you begin working for yourself.

What are the different ways of making money?

There are so many ways to make money but they all fall into the cashflow quadrant. The cashflow quadrant was created by Robert Kiyosaki and breaks up all forms of income into four categories. There are multiple attributes for each category but they focus on what is put in to produce income. Your income is not limited to one area at a time. None of these categories are a bad way to earn income but understanding your goals and lifestyle will help you pick income streams that best work for you.

Employment: You work for someone else to make money; income is a result of the value of your time and the amount time you work

Self-Employment: You work for yourself to make money; income is a result of the value of your product and the time you put into the making products

Business System: Other people and systems work for you to make you money; income is a result of the quality of your system and the value of your product

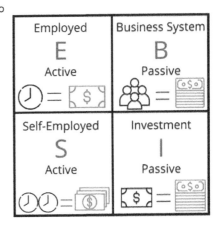

Investments: Your money works for you to make you money; income is a result of the value and performance of your investments

What is passive income?

Passive income is money that is earned with little to no effort compared to a traditional job. Passive income streams need to be built to a place where the income received is significant enough to partially or even completely replace your primary source of income.

Is there a way to earn income without working?

Yes, this is called passive income. Passive income generally comes from your assets as a percentage of the value of that asset. Some stocks pay dividends, bonds pay interest, and real estate can produce rent. By making consistent contributions to your investments, their value will reach a point where you can earn thousands of dollars in passive income. Out of the three I mentioned, real estate gives the highest return for your investment, but most of the rent is used to pay off the mortgage. It is possible to earn income without working, but you need to make an investment before you receive that income.

"Ask yourself 'How can I add more value to myself and to those around me?'"

How do I build multiple streams of income?

There are multiple ways to earn income and therefore multiple ways to have multiple income streams. The best way to go about it is picking the strategy that best fits your lifestyle. You can have multiple streams of income by having multiple jobs or by having a job and self-sustaining online business or by being self employed and owning rental properties or by having a side hustle while you work your normal job. You can try out different ways of earning income to see which best fits your lifestyle and then work on developing those streams to become more self-sustainable or to produce greater returns; this will oftentimes require greater up-front investment. Ideas for income streams are a regular 9-to-5 job, a weekend side hustle, an online business, real estate investing, or investing in bonds and dividend stocks.

What are all the major ways of earning passive income and what are the advantages/disadvantages of each?

Income Source	Advantages	Disadvantages
Bond Interest	- stable - essentially guaranteed	- need large investments
Stock Dividends	- can increase in value	- need large investments - not always guaranteed - can decrease in value
Rental Real Estate	- stable - increases over time - larger returns	- not completely passive - use income to pay mortgage
Creating a Product*	- potential to sell itself - potential for a lot of income	- marketing required - a lot of upfront work - not guaranteed - not always stable

a product only provides passive income after it's created and only if it is self-sustaining

Is being an entrepreneur a good way to earn money?
Entrepreneurship should not only be looked at as a way to earn money because there are much easier ways to earn money. You can earn money by being an entrepreneur but, oftentimes, it takes a while for you to not only see revenue but to actually profit from your business. Being an entrepreneur is both the job of an employer and an employee. In the short run, entrepreneurship may not be a good way to earn your primary income, but it can be a good way to earn money as a side hustle.

On average, how long does it take to start a business?

A business is started as soon as you decide that you'd like to provide a good or service to others. Once that's decided, you start planning what your product will be and how to market it. If you're asking how long it takes to register a business, it takes about 4 weeks. If you're asking how long it takes to turn a profit, that can be anywhere from 18 months to 3 years. There's a lot of hard work that goes on behind the scenes of a business to see tangible results, but a business starts when you've decided you want to start a business. When it'll become successful is another question that depends on different factors such as the demand in that market, your marketing, and what makes you unique.

Can you give examples of ways — other than a traditional job — that a college student can generate income? Ways that are not time-consuming and will hopefully prove valuable in the long-run?

Here is a list of some ways you can make money in your free time. Most of the jobs that increase your skills are online jobs, and your hours depend on the amount of work you're assigned and how skilled and efficient you are.

Online, more skill development
- Virtual assistant
- Social media manager
- Freelance writing
- Freelance design/media

In-person, more flexibility
- Ride-sharing/delivery driving (Uber, Lyft, Doordash, Postmates, etc.)
- Driving for dollars/birddogging *(check Real Estate section for details)*
- Tasks on demand (TaskRabbit, Agent Anything, etc.)

I know you make money based on how much you can give, but my question is how do you find out what you can give? Like how do you discover what people want/need, and how do you make it profitable?

A great way to discover what people are looking for is to pay attention to things people often complain about in conversation. Another way is by learning skills that you know everyone benefits from but few people actually have. If you have knowledge or a skill that addresses these areas of people's lives, you can either directly fix their problem by offering your services or teach people how they can fix the problem themselves and charge for that education. Chances are you'll find yourself in a market or industry where people have access to hundreds of options to fix their problem, so you then need to decide what makes you stand out from the rest and market yourself based on that difference.

How do I make money online the real way?

As a result of the growth of the internet in our everyday lives, there are so many ways to make money online, just like there are endless ways to make money in person. Some are more passive than others, and some require more time and skill to develop. With online employment, the limitation is on how much you're willing to learn and take advantage of. Here are a list of some ways you can make money through online means:

- Affiliate linking
- Ad sense on YouTube
- Social media brand deals
- Selling an online course
- Online tutoring
- Graphic design
- Media editing
- Being a virtual assistant
- Proofreading
- Having a blog and selling ad space on your website
- Web development
- Online distribution/wholesaling
- Content creation through subscription
- Social media manager
- Freelance writing

How to find remote work during the school year?

Two great platforms you can use to find remote jobs are Indeed and Handshake. Indeed is a job search site that matches employers and employees. The site matches based on your credentials, what you're looking for in a job, and what employers are looking for. Handshake is just like Indeed except it's geared towards college students and their professional level. It not only provides ideas for jobs but online career centers and other resources to help students find work during and after college. They both provide job listings you can apply for directly.

In the interest of building wealth, should salary be my top consideration when looking for employment?

Income is really important in the pursuit of building wealth but you also need to remember that you spend about half of your waking hours doing activities related to your job. Investment bankers have six-figure salaries but very intense work environments and struggle with work-life balance. You can also become wealthy on a lower salary with good money habits and a good budget, other roots of your financial life. Yes, consider the salary but also consider if the job will negatively impact your well-being as well. Your health — mental, emotional, and relational — are more important than the money you make.

"Learn skills that you know everyone benefits from but few people actually have"

Is how much I make really that important if I'm doing something I love and am passionate about?

Loving your job is great because of how much time you spend doing it but, if you're barely able to keep up with your expenses, you may want to reconsider your employment. We don't only find passion in our jobs. You can find passion in your relationships and your hobbies. The primary purpose of a job, as an employee, is to earn income and your job should be fulfilling that role. Also, if there's a conflict between your passion and your income, that thing you love could easily become something that stresses you out. Having a decently paying job that you're passionate about is amazing but don't suffer because you want to work in your passion.

Retaining Money

The Blueprint

Ada is a 27 year old nurse living in Houston, Texas. She got hair done every month, got her nails done every three weeks, and ate out with her friends twice a month. One day, as she was heading back from work, she noticed her check engine light turn on. When she took her car to the mechanic, she was told that she needed a new catalytic converter and her car was due for an emissions inspection soon. Ada didn't have a few hundred dollars to spare and quickly realized she needed to start saving more. She started wearing her natural hair out more often and invited her friends over to cook instead of going out to eat; the nails were a priority. She developed a habit of saving and found it really easy to start investing when her brother brought the idea up to her.

Besides not knowing what to do with their money, the reason a lot of people struggle with their finances is because they don't retain enough of their income. What's the purpose of money? To be spent. So what's wrong with people spending their money, if that's what it's meant for? There's nothing wrong with spending money; the problem is not spending it effectively.

Out of all the sections, this one is the most heavily affected by our habits and mindset towards money. Let me pose a question to you: how much of your income is truly yours? You may be inclined to say all of it, but then I'd ask you, "Well, doesn't some of it belong to your service provider, your utilities providers, the grocery store, the gas station, etc.?" After you finish paying everyone else, how much of your income is left? About 60% of Americans live paycheck to paycheck: none of their income is truly theirs.

Retaining your money is such a crucial part of a healthy financial life. You need to know how to pay yourself as you pay everyone else. This is achieved through budgeting, the blueprint of wealth. Budgeting helps you to truly be in control of your money instead of everyone else controlling it for you. This section addresses all things budgeting and gives you a framework to immediately begin controlling your money and to pay yourself. Healthy financial lives are developed through the structure of a budget.

What is budgeting?

Budgeting is simply categorizing how you want to spend your money by telling it where to go before you even spend it. Think of budgeting like planning. Just like it's best to have a plan before you go on vacation or when you go grocery shopping, it's best to have a plan for your money so you know exactly what to do with it. When most people hear the word "budget," their mind goes to lack of money. However, wealthy people are only wealthy because they budget.

Why is budgeting important?

The money that we get with each paycheck isn't really our money. It belongs to our service provider, our mortgage lender, our utility providers, our streaming services, the gas station, the grocery store, and, by the end of the month, we have no money for ourselves. Budgeting helps you to make sure you get paid while you pay everyone else. It helps you keep more of your money and also puts you in control of it. Instead of wondering where your entire paycheck goes at the end of each month, you'll tell it where to go before you even get it, and that includes your own pocket.

I generally know where I spend my money. Why do I need a budget?
Budgeting is not only for keeping track of where your money goes but also for planning for your future. Without a budget it's difficult to know how much you should be investing or saving to meet your goals. Also, your brain is not best used as storage. Having a budget will free up space in your mind for you to think, dream, and process more.

Isn't budgeting only for people who don't have enough money?
No, budgeting is a strategy that sustains and propels people in whatever financial situation. The word budgeting has a negative connotation in our society because it makes us feel like we can't use our money however we want; therefore, you would only need to budget if you didn't have enough money for your needs and wants. However, budgeting allows us to have more control over our money. Budgeting is the first practical step toward financial freedom because you evaluate where your money is going and then tell it where to go. For the average person, the only way to "have enough money" and to have more money is through budgeting.

"Wealthy people are only wealthy because they budget"

How do I budget effectively?
Effective budgeting is allocating and spending your money in a way that allows you to meet all your needs, invest in your future, and still live your life now. The first step to this is having the right categories within your budget. Your budget can be as specific or general as you want. Once you've established your categories, you need to put dollar amounts or income percentages to each category. The 50/30/20 model allocates 50% to your needs, including debt, 30% to your wants, and 20% to your savings

and investments. This is a good framework to start with, and you can adjust and expand as you wish. Once you've designated your allocations, the only thing left to do is be disciplined and stick to your budget. Your budget should reflect your current life situations, so let it be flexible enough to change as your life changes.

What are some good and easy budgeting strategies?
There are a countless number of budgeting strategies out there, each with their own pros and cons. Budgeting strategies can provide a framework for your own budget, but they don't need to be followed to a T. Budgeting is very individualized and is dependent on your current circumstances and values. For almost every strategy, you will need to decide your categories and the allocation for each. While reading these strategies, see which ones best suit your current lifestyle and goals.

Percentage Budgeting: allocating a certain percentage to different outlined categories. The most famous percentages are the 50/30/20 method: 50% necessities; 30% wants; 20% savings. Necessities include bills, groceries, gas, and debt. Savings include emergency, general savings, and investments. Wants are everything else.

Zero-Based: "spending" every single dollar by the end of the month. If the money you allocated for eating out is not completely spent by the end of the money, you put it into your savings or investments. The idea is to have no money unaccounted for at the end of each month.

Envelope Method: having an envelope with cash in it for each category; you can only spend the cash in that envelope for that category. Although we don't really use cash anymore, you can still use this method by having separate bank accounts and cards for each category.

Pay Yourself First: allocating money for your savings and investments before you pay anything else. Once you've set your savings and investment goals, you contribute to those categories before you pay your bills or debt each month. Essentially, you're prioritizing your money over other people's money.

Automatic: setting up automatic payments with your bank for your bills, debt, investments, and savings. For your investments and savings, you determine how much you want to contribute every month.

What categories should I have in my budget?
Your budgeting categories depend on what's important to you and where you tend to spend your money. Essential categories for everyone are:

- ❖ Emergencies
- ❖ Bills/Necessities
- ❖ Debt
- ❖ Spending

Categories to include to contribute to building wealth are

- ❖ Investments
- ❖ Savings

You should also include giving/charity in your budget. Each of these categories can be broken down further based on each person's life and circumstances: bills/necessities can include groceries, electricity, service providers; savings can include vacations, new cars, gifts; spending can include eating out, going out with friends, streaming services.

How do I determine my needs and wants within my budget?
Needs are things that we can't live without. There are our basic human needs and then there are our needs to function within our society. Our basic needs are food, water, shelter, and clothes. Our societal needs are transportation, a phone, and internet access. Everything else that isn't directly related to these needs is a want because you can live and function within society without it; it may be a really important want like a computer, therapy, or even your savings, but at the end of the day, you can still live without them. A lot of times we mistake our wants for needs and feel obligated to spend money on them. The only wants that should be treated

as needs are your savings and investments, and I would suggest including charity/giving as well.

What are all the things that could be in each category of my budget?

Savings
❖ Safety net
❖ Retirement account
❖ New Car
❖ House
❖ Vacation
❖ Any big purchase

Bills/Necessities
❖ Utilities
❖ Gas/transportation
❖ Service provider
❖ Groceries

Debt
❖ Student loans
❖ Car note
❖ Mortgage
❖ Credit cards
❖ Store cards

Misc. Spending
❖ Streaming services
❖ Eating out
❖ Movies
❖ Subscriptions
❖ Shopping
❖ Gifts
❖ Beauty maintenance
❖ Travel expenses
❖ Anything else

How can I reduce my expenses?

The best way to reduce expenses is cutting out things from your miscellaneous spending that won't have a negative effect on your overall well-being. You can also become more self-sufficient in some areas. Here are a few practical tips on how you can reduce your expenses.

❖ Pay off your debts early
❖ Meal prep to eat out less

- Set times of year to shop for clothes or shop at thrift stores
- Unsubscribe from the subscriptions you don't use
- Only subscribe to your most used streaming services
- Grocery shop with a list
- Learn to do beauty maintenance (nails, hair, haircuts, wax, etc.) yourself
- Do at home workouts or buy free weights to save on a gym membership

Can I change my budget or should it always be the same?
Your budget should change with your life circumstances. Your budget in college is not going to be the same as when you get a full-time job because your income has significantly increased. If you're planning to move or make a big purchase, your savings might increase. If you received a raise, you may consider increasing your investments. Your budget exists to reflect your life and your goals so if your life is changing significantly, your budget should change as well.

How many separate bank accounts should I have as a young adult seeking to manage my money better?
This all depends on how you decide to manage your money and how disciplined you are. In general, have separate emergency, general savings, and checking accounts. If you choose to do the envelope method of budgeting, then you'll have multiple accounts for different categories. If you know you're not as disciplined when it comes to spending, you can have an account for each of your major budgeting categories. Having different accounts makes it easier to see how much money is truly in each category. Some banks have service fees for checking accounts so, more accounts may mean more expenses but check your bank's policies.

How much of my money should I save versus investing? Like, after I put money down for priorities and necessities, is it safe to invest all of it, or should I always save a part for caution?

This is a great question. Many people either tend to save a bit too much or not save at all, so it's great to think about how to strike a balance between the two. There are two types of savings: emergency savings, or your safety net, and goal-oriented savings. You should always have a safety net of about three to six months worth of your expenses. If that's a large sum for you to save up, start with $1,000 and add $500 to your goal each time until you hit three months of your expenses. While you're building your safety net, invest. You don't need to wait until it's fully funded to begin investing. Once it is fully funded though, if you have no large short-term purchases you're saving for, invest the rest. The reason I say this is because interest rates on savings are lower than inflation, so your money is actually losing value over time sitting in the bank if you're not planning to use it soon. This is not to say that you shouldn't spend any money on things you want. Your wants should also be a factor in your budget.

"Meet all your needs, invest in your future, and live your life now"

How much should I have in savings?

The purpose of savings is to be prepared in case of an emergency. If you don't currently have any savings, start with creating a $1,000 emergency fund. Once you've reached $1,000, gradually increase the amount by $500 increments until you have up to three months worth of your expenses. This amount will sustain you in case anything happens to your source of income but will also be enough for you to draw from if any unexpected situations occur. If you do draw from your emergency fund for unexpected situations, remember to replenish it back to three months worth of your expenses.

What finance professionals do I need to manage my finances and when?
Accountant, bookkeeper etc.?

Generally, I think everyone should have a financial advisor/planner, an attorney, and possibly a tax accountant. A financial planner will help you to plan out your whole life financially and provide advice and a plan to achieve all of your financial goals. These can be one-time interactions or long-term relationships, but I suggest developing a long-term relationship with a financial planner. Typically, a financial plan can range anywhere from $2000 - $5000, so it's best to visit one when you have disposable income and a more complex financial life.

An attorney is useful in your financial journey for drawing up wills, trusts, and estate plans. They come in handy once you have a family and when your assets are growing to a sizable amount. Wills, trusts, and estate plans are all legal documents, and attorneys will ensure that all the legal information of your asset transfers is included in the document and clearly communicated.

A tax accountant files your taxes for you and works with you to help reduce your tax liability wherever possible. Most people don't need tax accountants because their tax situations are simple, but, for people who have multiple streams of income, are self-employed, or have high cash-flowing investments, a tax accountant will be really beneficial for your financial life. This is another long-term financial relationship you'll have once established.

Other financial professionals you can seek out are financial coaches, insurance agents, or debt counselors, depending on your life situations. Financial coaches help you get your finances under control and understand your relationship with money. Insurance agents help you find the best insurance for you and your family. Debt counselors are specifically trained to help you get out and stay out of crippling debt. Financial planners and tax accountants can offer bookkeeping services as well. Every financial professional comes with a fee, so really be mindful of what professionals would add the most value to your life.

Should everyone have a financial advisor? What do they do that I can't do for myself?

I believe everyone should have a financial advisor, just like everyone should have a doctor. Just as doctors are trained in medicine, financial advisors are professionally trained in finances and know exactly what to look for when assessing your finances and your goals. They offer you specialized advice and strategies because they have in-depth knowledge about the financial industry. You could be your own financial advisor if you knew all the areas to examine in your finances and the solutions to problem areas. It takes a lot of studying to learn everything and most people don't have the time or resources to fully learn about personal finance; there is information online but it's scattered all over the internet and difficult to know what is truly relevant. Financial advisors do charge for their services and the fees can be very hefty because they're doing a lot of work, but educating yourself in the meantime will suffice, especially if your financial situation is fairly simple. Once you do have the money, I suggest developing a long-term relationship with an advisor so you can better plan your finances.

"Always replenish your emergency fund when you draw from it"

When I'm saving money, what am I saving for?

There are two main types of savings: emergency savings and goal-oriented savings. Emergency savings are exactly what they sound like, savings that will be used only in the case of an emergency i.e. job loss, medical expenses, or family troubles. Goal-oriented savings, also self-explanatory, are savings that will be used towards a certain goal like buying a new car, making a down payment on a house, or going on vacation. You should always have an emergency savings of three to six months of your expenses, but you won't always need goal-oriented savings.

Should I have different accounts for my different expense categories?
This strategy is specifically called envelope budgeting, and it works best for people who struggle with overspending. Not everyone needs to have different accounts for their different expense categories, but if you feel like you struggle with being disciplined in your spending, then this might be a good strategy for you to start budgeting. Once you feel you've developed the habit, you can go some months on a few accounts to see how you do: if you've improved, you can reduce the number of accounts; if you still struggle with overspending, continue with the envelope method. One thing about having many accounts is that some banks charge service fees for checking accounts, and the more accounts you have open, the more fees you pay.

How often should I review my budget?
There are different reasons for needing to review your budget. Review your budget two to four times a month to see if you're actually sticking to it. Review every three months to check on your savings and investing goals and adjust when needed. At least once a year, you should review your budget to see if it's reflective of your current life situations.

How do I create a realistic budget?
A realistic budget is one that accurately reflects where your life is now and where you want your life to be in the future. For your life now, start by reviewing all your purchases and payments from the past three to four months to see if there's a pattern in your spending. Calculate what percentage of your money goes to your necessities, what percentage goes to debt payments, and what percentage goes to miscellaneous purchases. If you already contribute to savings and investments, you're on the right path. For your necessities, determine if this amount is too much and look for ways you can reasonably reduce your expenses. Next, reduce the amount of miscellaneous spending by redirecting that money to create a $1,000 safety net; this can take place over a few months. Once you have

your safety net, increase your contributions to savings and investing. Build up your safety net to at least three months worth of your expenses and start investing in index funds.

While you're building up a habit of investing, review your life goals and how much money it'll take to achieve and sustain them. The specific investments you make will depend on what you want to do with that money in the future, but a good rule of thumb for young people is to invest in funds that mimic the market and growth funds because you will see a lot of long-term appreciation.

What is the wisest methodology of budgeting and how does this change based on stage of life/age/place on the financial ladder?

The wisest budgeting methodology is percentage budgeting because every other budgeting method stems from it and it's very flexible. With percentage budgeting, you can start by looking up percentages and categories that have worked for other people, and as you build your budgeting habit you can customize to better fit your life. You can be as specific or as general as you'd like, which leaves room for flexibility as your financial situations change. Here are some examples of how your percentages might change as your life changes:

- ❖ **Getting a raise:** increased investing percentage

- ❖ **Getting married:** increased necessities percentage, might introduce a category for date nights, increased safety net

- ❖ **Buying a house:** increased savings percentage, decreased spending percentage

- ❖ **Having a child:** increased safety net, increased food expenses, decreased spending percentage, introduce categories for child care

46

How do I curate savings if the interest rates at banks are < 1% for savings accounts?

As mentioned earlier, savings exist for short-term use, whether that's in case of unexpected events or for an upcoming purchase. They need to be readily accessible and, as a result, interest rates on them aren't as important because they are not investments. However, if you want to save with a higher return, you can invest in the money market and short-term bonds. Bonds pay periodic interest, so you will be making money on your investment until the maturity date. The money market is a hyper-short-term bond market, usually six months or less, for banks and corporations. Money market instruments usually don't pay interest but they're usually posted at a discount, so you'll get back more than what you put in. There are penalties for trying to redeem debt securities early, so I would NEVER recommend using this strategy for your safety net (*check out the "Money Market" section of Bonds for more information*).

"When you make more money, invest more"

When should I use my emergency fund?

It's good to first determine what an emergency really is. If it can have a significant effect on your most basic human needs — your life, your health, your shelter, your provision/income or that of your immediate family — then it's an emergency. Unexpected situations can be a car repair, pipe leakage, or helping out a loved one, and these can also be factored into your emergency fund. By saving up three to six months worth of your expenses, you have enough for unexpected situations and for emergencies. Remember to always replenish your emergency fund whenever you draw from it.

How should my budget change once I start making more money?

When you make more money, invest more. Most people are inclined to increase their spending when their income increases, but the first thing to increase should be your investments. If you have debt, you can split that increase between your investments and debt repayment. Lifestyle changes should accompany situational changes like getting married, moving to a new city, or having kids. Also, with increased income comes a value increase for each part of your budget, so you could be spending more but also investing more than you were before.

Investing

Demystifying Wealth Creation

Emeka, 25 years old, sees a lot of people on Instagram and TikTok who talk about making thousands of dollars in a week through the stock market. He's been thinking about investing, and seeing these people encourages him, but he's uncertain about where to start and if what they say is true or just clickbait. He decided to talk to his cousin — who's been investing since he was 18 — who advised him to invest at least $100 into the QQQ index fund each month. They continue to have conversations about investing and always share their strategies and things they're learning with each other. They even got their younger sisters, who are 19 and 21, to start investing.

Cryptocurrency; index funds; GameStop; market crash; S&P 500; Forex; diversification; the stonks. What does any of this mean, and why does it get people so excited? Many people have heard of the stock market and know it as a way that those Wall Street guys make their money. All the jargon and advertising of the potential to make large sums of money makes investing feel as inaccessible as buying a private jet. The reality is investing is actually as accessible as having a spare $10 in your bank account.

There's an overwhelming amount of information on the internet about the stock market and investing, and beginners seeking out this information are often left more confused than when they started. A lot of investing information on social media is used to create an emotional reaction to get you excited about making more money without the real tools of how to do so. There's also a lot of people that advertise quick cash, which costs their followers a lot of money. With so much information and so many different agendas and opinions, how can people know where to begin and who to trust?

The information I provide in this book is reliable and accurate investing advice for everyone, but how can you trust that? For one, I'm a licensed investment advisor. The country recognizes me as a reliable source for investment advice. Also, my primary goal is to demystify investing and to create accessible, understandable information that gives you the confidence to start investing as soon as possible. I'm not going to tell you how to flip your money; in fact, I focus on delaying your gratification to build long-term wealth. I explain the mechanics of investing and the purpose and intention behind investing so you can go in with the right expectations. I break investing down into the simplest terms and recommend strategies to help you start investing now. My goal is to make investing a walk in the park, so without further ado, let's conquer this mountain.

What is an investment?
An investment is the sacrifice of a current asset — time, money, effort — in the hopes of an increase in value over time. With a monetary investment, you're hoping to get out more money than you put in by sacrificing the use of that money for the time it's invested. Returns on most investments are not guaranteed but can be expected given the history and current state of the economy.

Why do people invest?

People invest to have a source of income outside of a traditional job. Most people will use this source during their retirement when they no longer want to work. Others will use it as a way to earn some passive income before retirement. Investing is one way in which people create wealth for themselves and their future generations.

What is principal?

Principal is the initial amount of money used to make an investment; it's the money you put in. There's also a principal in debt, and it's the original amount of the loan you took out: the money the creditor "invests" in you. It's the amount of money on which interest accrues.

What is simple growth?

Simple growth is the constant increase in the value of your original investment, the principal. Usually expressed as a percentage, simple growth is always calculated on the principal; graphically the slope of a line is the simple growth rate. If you invest $1,000 with a simple growth rate of 5%/yr, each year your investment would grow by $50. In investments, simple growth usually shows up in bonds in the form of interest payments.

What is compound growth?

Compound growth is growth on growth or increase on top of increase. Just like simple growth happens on the principal, compound growth happens on both the principal and the growth from each period. Essentially, the principal amount resets each period, unlike simple growth where the principal amount remains the same. Using the same example, a $1,000 investment with a 5%/yr compound growth rate will increase by $50 in the first year. In the second year, the principal becomes $1,050, and the increase that year will be $52.50. In the third year, the principal will be $1,102.50, and the increase will be $55.13. Each year, the growth increases and causes your investment to rise at faster and faster rates. Most investments increase with compound growth.

Is there really much of a difference between simple growth and compound growth?

There's a huge difference between simple growth and compound growth. In the graph below, a one-time investment of $1,000 is growing at a rate of 10% for both simple and compound growth. In the beginning years, the growth difference seems small but as more years pass, the growth becomes incomparable.

Compound vs. Simple Growth

Why is time so important in investing?

Time is so crucial because the magic of compound growth is completely dependent on time. The graph for the previous question shows that compound growth has more effect the longer money is invested.
Something to remember is that most of your investments will be used decades down the line, and compound growth will have more to work with if investments are made earlier. Here's another example of the importance of time on compound interest in investing.

Years Invested	Yearly Contribution	Yearly Growth (10%)	
1	$1,000	$100	
2	$1,000	$210	
3	$1,000	$331	
4	$1,000	$464	
5	$1,000	$611	
6	$1,000	$772	
7	$1,000	$949	
8	**$1,000**	$1,144	growth > 1x contribution
9	$1,000	$1,358	
10	$1,000	$1,594	
11	$1,000	$1,853	
12	**$1,000**	$2,138	growth > 2x contribution
13	$1,000	$2,452	
14	$1,000	$2,797	
15	**$1,000**	$3,177	growth > 3x contribution
16	$1,000	$3,595	
17	**$1,000**	$4,054	growth > 4x contribution
18	$1,000	$4,560	
19	**$1,000**	$5,116	growth > 5x contribution
20	$1,000	$5,727	

After eight years, the growth of your investment is more than your contribution that year. Four years later, it's more than twice your contribution. Two years later, it's more than three times your contribution. As you continue to contribute, the yearly growth continues to increase at higher and higher rates.

What is the Rule of 72?

The Rule of 72 is a quick analysis trick used to determine the performance of an investment over time. By dividing 72 by the constant compound growth rate of an investment, you get the number of years it will take for that investment to double without further contributions. An investment with a growth rate of 5% will take about 14.5 years to double; a growth rate of 7% will take a little over 10 years to double; a growth rate of 10% will take a little over 7 years to double. Investing $1,000 at a rate of 10%/yr will take 7 years to become $2,000 but will become $4,000, not $3,000, in another 7 years, and $8,000 in another 7 years. The Rule of 72 demonstrates the significance of time when it comes to investing; the earlier you invest the better.

What is an investment fund?

An investment fund is a pool of money used to make investments for multiple contributors. Investment funds are used for people who have similar investing interests or goals to combine their efforts. They can be managed or traded on the stock market like stocks (Exchange-Traded Funds/ETFs).

Are funds better investments than individual investments?

Yes, funds are much better investments than individual investments, or stock picking, for two main reasons: diversification and professional knowledge. Funds use the pooled money to invest in multiple different companies, which spreads the risk of one company across many. With stock picking, your investments are subject to the risks that each company faces. Many funds are managed by professional stock analysts so they can pick the best stocks for the goals of that fund. Picking stocks requires knowing how to analyze a company's books and understanding the market that company is in. Doing this for multiple companies is literally a full-time job, and by investing in funds, you give that responsibility over to the professionals. Most funds do have management fees, except for ETFs, whereas individual stocks don't.

How can I be strategic as a new investor?

To be strategic, you need a strategy, and to have a strategy, you need an end goal. Being strategic as an investor starts with knowing what your financial goals are because that'll determine what kinds of investments you'll make. In general, good investing strategies for young people are to invest in index funds and growth funds. As a young person, most of your investments are going to be used 20+ years down the line, and you want to have as much capital appreciation as possible. Investing goals that focus on high appreciation are also riskier, but you're able to take the risk at this stage of your life as long as your savings and necessities are already covered. Investing in funds also provides more risk management because of diversification.

> *"Diversify; don't put all your eggs in one basket"*

How should I go about investing? Is it too early to start? How much money do I need to start?

It's never too early to start investing; the earlier the better actually. There is no minimum amount to start investing in the stock market, specifically because of fractional shares. In decades past, you would have had to buy whole shares of stocks and have enough money to buy at least one share of any given stock. Now, because of new technology, you can buy fractional shares of any stock, which allows you to invest any dollar amount into stocks. If you have $10 and don't know what to do with it, throw it into an index fund.

When you're investing, you need to have a long-term mentality and consistency in your contributions no matter what the market looks like. Investing is a long-term game, and trying to flip your money can get you into a lot of trouble. Consistently invest into index funds, and, if it fits your budget, increase the amount of money you're investing whenever you can.

How much do I need to know before I start investing?

Before you make your first investment, you need to know what a stock is, what an index fund is, and what causes price changes in the stock market. It's good to be educated on the things you're investing in so you make better investment decisions, but you don't need to be a stock analyst before you can invest. You'll learn a lot along your financial journey that'll affect your future investment strategies, but all you need to know to get started are the very basics of stocks and index funds.

Why is cryptocurrency such a big deal?

Cryptocurrency has a lot of hype surrounding it because it's a new form of money, and it could be the standard form of exchange in the future. Think about how we use money for almost everything in our life and then imagine completely switching to cryptocurrency. It's like the evolution from paper money to cards and checks to online transfers and payments. Even with that evolution, we're still using the same currency, but cryptocurrency is a whole new currency that can be universal instead of geographical.

What's all this crypto and bitcoin stuff about? Is it real? Is it wise to invest in it?

A lot of the talk in society surrounding cryptocurrency is speculation and projection. It is very possible that cryptocurrency could become the primary mode of exchange in the future, but a lot of investing talk around it is speculation. Cryptocurrency is a currency like the euro, the dollar, or the yen, and "investing" in crypto is really just changing your money to another currency in hopes that its value will increase relative to your domestic currency. Currency values are a result of a country's internal economic status, and since cryptocurrency is decentralized — not associated with a single economy — it's hard to determine its real value.

On top of that, it's not widely used as a mode of exchange. I think cryptocurrency can be a fun thing to invest in and watch over time, but let it be your last consideration when making investment decisions.

What is diversification?

Diversification is the allocation of your investments in multiple different asset classes to reduce the effect of risk from any one asset: essentially not putting all your eggs in one basket. You can diversify among asset classes, and you can also diversify within a certain asset class. You can invest in real estate, stocks, and bonds, and within your stock investments you can diversify through dividend stocks, growth stocks, and value stocks.

"Being strategic as an investor starts with knowing what your financial goals are"

Can you rank investments based on their risk?

I will answer this question based on the idea that risk is the probability of depreciation of the principal value of the asset. For the three most widely used asset classes — stocks, bonds, and real estate — from safest to riskiest is bonds, real estate, then stocks. For most bonds, the value at which you buy the bond is the value at which it's redeemed. They don't face appreciation or depreciation unless clearly stated, and you receive steady income from them. Real estate values do fluctuate, but they don't have great volatility, and property values always increase in the long run. There are a plethora of stocks out there and different types of stocks have different risks, but overall, stocks are riskier than bonds and real estate because appreciation, or even principal retention, is not guaranteed. There are ways to pick stocks that are almost guaranteed to increase in value over time, and their comparative risk should not be the reason you don't invest in them, because they are the most accessible of the asset classes.

What are different investment strategies?

Most investment strategies are grouped into three categories: aggressive, conservative, and moderate. All strategies are looking for long-term growth, but their methods of achieving them differ.

Aggressive strategies strive for growth first and foremost and, as a result, are the riskiest investments; they have both really high returns and really big losses, especially in the short run. Aggressive strategies are more sensitive to economic cycles and can outpace the market in periods of growth and decline. People who are risk takers tend to use aggressive strategies.

Conservative strategies look for ways to minimize loss and maintain stability; their growth tends to be very stable but with lower rates. Unlike aggressive strategies, they don't react as much to economic cycles and, as a result, have lower rates of growth and decline. These strategies are used by people who'll need their money in less than five years.

Moderate strategies are a mix of the aggressive and conservative approaches. They aim for growth while trying to minimize risk based on the investor's risk tolerance; there's usually more aggressive investments than conservative. For more risk taking investors, they may have a 75/25 split in aggressive and conservative investments while a risk averse investor may have a 60/40 split. These strategies tend to follow economic cycles and have slightly higher or lower rates of growth and decline depending on the allocation. Most investors use moderate strategies.

When determining which strategy is best for you, look at when you'll need the money and how much risk you're willing to take for growth. Aggressive strategies are recommended for long-term growth (20+ years), but some people are more emotionally affected by economic downturns and feel better with more moderate strategies.

What's an asset class?

An asset class is a group of investments that have similar characteristics. The asset classes are cash (bank investments), equities (stocks), fixed income (bonds), real estate, and alternative investments. People invest in these different classes for diversification and because each class has its own risk and benefits. Just like different classes in school contribute to your education in different ways, each asset class contributes to your financial life in its own unique way.

What's a mutual fund?

Mutual funds are actively managed and traded investment funds. You can invest in mutual funds by buying shares from the fund. When you buy, you pay the price of the share plus other charges. A management fee is taken out of your investment each year which reduces the real return you see. Since mutual funds are actively managed, they have a prospectus which has information about the funds investment strategies, their past performance, and the fees. You can pick mutual funds based on your investment goals and the different strategies they employ.

What's the difference between a mutual fund and an ETF?

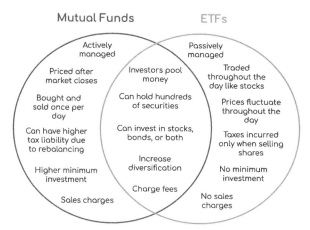

Mutual Funds — ETFs

Mutual Funds:
- Actively managed
- Priced after market closes
- Bought and sold once per day
- Can have higher tax liability due to rebalancing
- Higher minimum investment
- Sales charges

Both (overlap):
- Investors pool money
- Can hold hundreds of securities
- Can invest in stocks, bonds, or both
- Increase diversification
- Charge fees

ETFs:
- Passively managed
- Traded throughout the day like stocks
- Prices fluctuate throughout the day
- Taxes incurred only when selling shares
- No minimum investment
- No sales charges

What are some really good, universal investment strategies?

- ❖ Invest in funds
- ❖ Dollar-cost averaging
- ❖ Use aggressive and moderate strategies until you're seven years out from retirement
- ❖ Have at least one real estate property
- ❖ Start ASAP

Can't I take more risk with my investments since I'm young?
You can technically take more risk because you won't need the money for a few decades, but make sure your risks are educated and not impulsive. There is more reward, or returns, associated with higher risk investments, but the risk of loss also increases. A smart way to take more risk is to use an aggressive investment strategy. The funds you choose based on this strategy will have professionally picked stocks that have good grounding and could give you higher returns in the long run. Do not take risks with money that is not budgeted for investments, and even with your investment money, use professionally chosen strategies.

Stocks

What is a stock?
A stock is a certificate of partial ownership within a public company. When companies go public, they issue stock so they can raise capital to expand their business operations. When you invest in stock, you are directly helping to grow a company. As the value of the company increases, your equity — cash — increases because your ownership is worth more.

What is common stock?
Common stock is stock that has voting rights and the ability to appreciate in value; this is what most people are referring to when they say the word "stock." Being an owner in the company means you have the right to vote

on decisions being made by the company. There are some companies that issue dividends to their common stockholders but not every company does.

What is preferred stock?

Preferred stock is stock that has priority claims over common stock and normally issues quarterly dividends but usually has no voting rights or appreciation potential. Priority claims means that if a company were to dissolve, preferred stockholders would receive their share of the company before common stockholders.

What is market capitalization?

Market capitalization is the dollar value of all of a company's shares. It's often used to determine the size of a company and its importance within the economy. There are small-cap ($300 mil. - $2 bil.), mid-cap ($2 bil. - $10 bil.), and large-cap companies($10 bil.+). Small-cap companies tend to be riskier investments, and they tend to be growth companies along with mid-cap companies. Large-cap companies tend to be really stable, well-known companies, and most dividend stocks are from large-cap companies.

What is a dividend?

A dividend is a distribution of a company's profit to its shareholders. Instead of reinvesting profits back into the company, they are distributed to the owners. They are paid periodically each year at a percentage of the stock price. Dividend yields normally range from 0% - 6% of the stock price, and yields in the 2% - 6% range are considered good investments. Since dividend payout is dependent on the price of the stock, dividend income can fluctuate from year to year.

Which stocks typically have dividends?

Larger and older companies tend to pay dividends. Dividends send a message that a company's finances are stable and that operations are able to continue even with no reinvestment. However, high dividend yield is normally a sign that the company's share price has dropped and the dividend might be reduced or revoked in the near future.

What are income stocks?

Income stocks are stocks that issue dividends to their stockholders. Usually stocks of stable, old companies are good income stocks because they have to have higher dividend rates than newer companies.

"A lot of wealth in our economy would not exist without the stock market"

What are growth stocks?

Growth stocks are stocks of companies whose main objective is growth. Stocks of newly public companies are classified as growth stocks. They don't typically pay dividends (or pay them at a very low rate) because their profits are being reinvested back into the company for further growth. They have the potential to have higher returns than the rest of the market but that also means they have the potential to have much lower returns.

What are value stocks?

Value stocks are stocks that appear to be underpriced based on the strength of the company's books (their assets). The book analysis shows that this company is of more value than its current price, making it a good investment because the price is expected to rise to its true value.

What are speculative stocks?

Speculative stocks are stocks that don't really have an established track record or books. As a result, they are very risky investments because not much analysis can be done on them to determine their worth. They tend to be brand new companies or companies where the hype doesn't match their books i.e. GameStop and AMC in 2021.

How are stocks priced?

The things that contribute to the price of a stock are the business' fundamentals, supply, and demand. Fundamentals generally determine prices long term and supply and demand determine them in the short term. When a company goes public, they have an IPO (initial public offering), which is the original price per share of their stock; all changes happen off of this price. A business' fundamentals are their earnings in relation to their market cap (number of shares and price per share). The most common way stock prices are determined is through the P/E (price-earnings) ratio. It is the price of a share divided by the company's earnings per share or the market cap divided by the company's earnings. This ratio is compared against the P/E ratio of similar companies or the industry ratio; higher ratios are seen to be overvalued and lower ratios undervalued. It's expected that over time the stock's P/E ratio will move toward the industry P/E.

The supply and demand effect on stocks is the same as its effect on anything else: increased demand and/or decreased supply leads to higher prices; decreased demand and/or increased supply leads to lower prices. Supply is the number of investors who want to sell their shares, and demand is the number of investors who want to buy shares. Factors that affect supply and demand are news and media, investor sentiments, and general economic performance (inflation, recession, etc.).

How exactly do I invest in stocks?

You can invest in stocks through a stock broker. You create an account with the broker, provide your bank information and some other personal information, and voila! You have access to the stock market. Your brokerage account will be connected to your bank account, but you need to add money to the brokerage account to invest in the stock market. Once you add money, you can start placing orders either on shares or with a dollar amount. The broker will execute the order and issue your stock. You should be able to see your stock, the number of shares, and the value of those shares.

What should regular people know about the stock market?
Important things to know about the stock market to be able to invest wisely are what stocks are, types of stocks, what determines and affects share prices, economic cycles, and what funds and dividends are. Having information on these areas makes it easier to know whether or not you're making sound investment decisions for your goals.

Why is the stock market important?
The stock market is important because it allows both companies and investors to raise and make money, respectively, in a very accessible way. Companies can raise money for their production without going into more debt, and investors can build wealth in a very hands-off way while contributing to companies they believe in. It's a staple in our free market, and, without it a lot of wealth in our economy would not exist.

What are the advantages of stocks?
Probably the biggest advantage of stocks is the appreciation potential, the ability for your investments to increase in value over time. The economy tends to grow at an average rate of 10% a year over a 10-year period, and this is much higher than inflation which tends to be at 2% a year. Also, the growth is compounded, which means that, if you look at your investments over time, they will likely have the shape of an exponential equation. This means when you take your money out, you're likely to get significantly more than you put in, even adjusted for inflation. This principle only really applies for long-term investing though.

Is investing in the stock market like gambling?

Not necessarily. While the stock market is uncertain, especially in the short run, we have confidence in its long-term performance given its consistent historical performance. You can gamble in the stock market if you don't know what you're doing, but if you take a little time to learn about it, you'll no longer be gambling but investing. All investments come with a certain risk, but the risks are calculated and based on concrete, measurable information.

Is the stock market the only way to invest?

While it is the most common and most well known, the stock market is only one way of investing. Other common ways of investing are bonds and real estate, which can also be invested in through the stock market. Alternative investments include gold and other metals, commodity derivatives, foreign markets, and currencies.

What's a stock broker?

A stock broker is a person or a company that is licensed to execute stock trades for investors. Many brokerages offer services outside of transaction such as advice, management, and education. TD Ameritrade, Charles Schwabb, Fidelity, E-Trade, SoFi, and Vanguard are some of the most widely used brokerages in the US.

How do I pick a good stock broker?

In general, stock brokers provide trading services, funds, and analysis and education tools; some even provide advisory services. You can't go wrong by investing through Fidelity, TD Ameritrade, or Charles Scwabb. They have fantastic educational and analysis tools, good screening services to help you reach your investing goals, and offer commission-free online trades.

Is Robinhood a good place to invest in stocks?

Robinhood is a reliable place to invest in the stock market. They've created a platform that makes stock investment more accessible to the general public in that it's very user and beginner friendly, and they don't charge commissions on transactions. They have resources for analysis, but because it's geared toward accessibility, their analysis tools aren't as detailed as more established brokers. If you're more into analysis, you can still use Robinhood to make transactions and use other systems for analysis.

Should I invest when markets are rising or falling?

Yes. You should always be investing, no matter what the markets look like. This strategy is called dollar-cost averaging. Markets are constantly rising and falling, and if you try to ride the wave, you might end up losing money you couldn't have predicted; you can never be sure when stock prices will drop and for how long. Dollar-cost averaging also helps to reduce emotional investing and allows your portfolio to consistently grow. Here's an example of the benefits of dollar-cost averaging.

Which stocks should I invest in?

I advise investing in funds over individual stocks because funds provide diversification and professional selection. In terms of picking funds, you want to look at what your investing goals are and pick funds based on them. Generally, index funds are good way to go, and some good index funds to invest in are Vanguard's S&P 500 ETF (VOO), Invesco QQQ Trust ETF (QQQ), SPDR S&P 500 ETF Trust (SPY), and Vanguard Total Stock Market ETF (VTI).

Should I invest in individual stocks?

I would not recommend investing in individual stocks because I'm a proponent of diversification, and it's very hard to diversify while investing in individual stocks. Individual stocks only represent one company and are not representative of anything outside of that company. While industry leaders can have an effect on and be semi-representative of their respective markets, they are still only one company at the end of the day. You also take on more risk when investing in individual stocks because the risk of that one company is directly linked to your investment performance.

How long should I invest in the stock market?

You should be invested in the stock market as long as you're alive. Investing is a long-term game, and you benefit more the longer you stay in the market. Even in retirement, the strategy is to gradually deplete your assets, not to take them all out at once.

How do I make money from stocks?

There are multiple ways to make money in the stock market, but they all stem from trading and investing. Trading is short term, usually less than one year, while investing is long term, usually longer than five years. Trading follows the "buy low, sell high" motto because it's focused on the short-term trends of the market; you enter the market when it's relatively low in the hopes of exiting when it increases to make a profit. Investing is the "buy and hold" method where you're relying on the general increase in the market over time to make your profit. Generally, with stocks you don't actually have access to the money until you sell. The main way you can receive cash without selling is by investing in dividend stock and preferred stock.

Another strategy to make money from stocks is by selling call options, AKA making a covered call. A call option is the ability to buy 100 shares of a stock at a given price, the strike price, if the stock's price goes up before a certain date, the expiration date. In order to have this option, the buyer pays a premium to the potential seller of the shares, which would be you in this case; you need to have 100 shares in order to sell a call option. If the option expires — meaning the option buyer doesn't buy the shares — you've collected the premium as income and get to keep your shares. If the option buyer fulfills their option and buys the shares, you've still collected the premium and can simply buy your shares back. Options with longer expiration dates have higher premiums.

"You should always be investing, no matter what the markets look like"

How do I know what to invest in?
As I always say, start by assessing your goals and look to funds. Determining which funds to invest in is a matter of choosing between an aggressive and a moderate investment strategy. Speaking with an advisor can help to make the best decision for you. For ETFs, you can research which funds best fit your strategy to make a decision. The important thing is that you come to a conclusion and don't experience analysis paralysis. Investing in something will always be a good idea, and you can always transfer your investments once you've learned more.

How often should I check my investments?

Truthfully, for long term investments you don't need to be checking them frequently because you're relying on long-term market trends for growth. However, that's unrealistic because we get curious about how our money's doing. If you feel inclined to check your investments, I would suggest reviewing them only 1 - 3 times a year, so every 4, 6 or 12 months. Constantly checking the market will make your emotions subject to the ever-changing cycles and may cause you to make some decisions that actually hurt your investments. When you go to check your investments, check only for performance and not to make a decision about whether or not to sell.

Are there funds for dividends?

Yes, there are funds that specifically invest in dividend stocks and provide dividends throughout the year. Just like with any other investment, you want to check their performance to know how much you'll be receiving and if it's a good investment for you.

Are stocks a good way to earn passive income?

You can earn passive income with stocks, but it takes a lot of capital (money) to get to the point where the income is passive. The most common way of earning passive income from stocks is through dividends, and the average dividend yield ranges from 2% - 4%. To receive $10k of passive income a year, you would need to have at least $500k invested in dividend stocks, and you can't touch that $500k either. It is possible to earn passive income from stocks, but you need to understand your motivation for receiving passive income and that it will take a lot of capital to see meaningful returns.

Is trading a good way to make money?

Trading is a great way to make money, only if you know exactly what you're doing. Trading relies on the fluctuations of stocks and the market, and in order to know when to buy and sell, you need to know technical analysis, which is reading stock charts. There are many different ways of trading, each of them using different analysis methods. You can make a lot of money trading, but you can also lose a lot of money as well. My advice is to establish your investment portfolio and other streams of income before you start trading, and once you do, only use a very small percentage of your investment money that you're willing to lose completely to trade.

Are stocks the best way to get money outside of a traditional job?

No, they are not. The purpose of stock investment is to build your assets so you have money to draw from in retirement and so you have assets to pass on to your kids. Most stocks don't provide income, and the ones that do require a lot of investment to see reasonable income. If you're looking for investments that can serve as another source of income, look into bonds, real estate, and side hustles.

"The best ways to invest are through ETFs or mutual funds"

Can I replace my income with enough stocks?

With enough stocks, yes, but enough might be $2.5 million worth. Income from stocks comes through dividends, and dividend yields range from 2% - 4%. 2% of $2.5 million is $50k. Better investments with higher return rates to replace your income are real estate and bonds.

How do I lose the least amount of money in the stock market?

There is no explicit answer for this because you could lose any amount of money in the stock market at any time because we can't determine what will happen to a company or the economy in the future. You can minimize your risk by investing in value stocks, dividend stocks, and old and large companies. These companies tend to have strong financials, so it's less likely they'll experience significant declines outside of market declines. You can also invest in bond ETFs, which tend to be pretty stable. My advice though is to not go into the stock market asking "how do I lose the least amount of money?" but rather "how can I have the most long-term growth?" There will eventually come a time when your stocks are decreasing in value, and if you're more focused on your losses than your long-term gains, you may make a decision that'll really hurt your investing goals.

Is it easy to take my money out of the market?
Yes: all you have to do to access your money is sell shares of the stocks you own. The stock market is open from 9 am to 4 pm EST, so if you sell outside of that window you'll have to wait until the market opens again for your trade to go through. It may take a few days for you to be able to transfer the money back to your account.

Should I sell my stocks when the market goes down or crashes?
No, market declines and crashes are part of the economic cycle, and they always turn around in the long run. It's actually more logical to invest more during a downturn; you're buying shares at a cheaper price, and they'll experience more appreciation. With long-term investing, it's advised to make steady investment contributions no matter what the market looks like

What's a stock index?
A stock index measures the performance of the stock market, or a subset of the stock market, by tracking the performance of selected stocks meant to represent that market. They are used to measure the overall performance of the economy and sectors within the economy and by investors to see how their investments are performing relative to the general market. Many portfolio managers try to make investments that beat a certain index.

What is the S&P 500?
The S&P 500 is a stock index that tracks America's 500 largest companies. It's commonly used to determine the state of the market and economy.

What is the list of stock indices?

There are about 5,000 indices for the US stock market but here are some of the most famous ones.

S&P 500: tracks the 500 largest American stocks

Dow Jones Industrial Average (DJIA): tracks 30 large-cap, blue-chip (strong financials) stocks

NASDAQ: tracks about 3,000+ tech-oriented stocks

Russell 2000: tracks 2,000 small-cap stocks

Wilshire 5000: tracks all American stocks

EAFE: tracks 1000+ stocks from 21 developed countries across Eurasia and Australia

S&P Mid-Cap 400: tracks 400 mid-cap companies

Which index best reflects the market?

The Wilshire 5000 is the best representation of how the stock market's performing because it represents almost every company in the market and each company's relative size within the market as well. The S&P 500 is another great indicator because the 500 companies it tracks represent 80% of the total US market cap.

Can I invest in an index?

You can't directly invest in an index because it's not a company, but you can invest in index funds. Index funds attempt to make investments in a way that mimics the performance of a particular stock index; some funds even try to beat the performance of certain indices. A lot of index funds are ETFs, exchange-traded funds, and can be invested directly in stock exchanges, just like you would invest in companies.

How do I know which index to invest in?

Picking what to invest in is always dependent on what your goals are and how much risk you're willing to take. It doesn't hurt to make investments into multiple indices to increase your market exposure and diversification. You can also invest in indices that track markets you're interested in or that you believe in; if you really like natural resources, you can invest in Vanguard Materials ETF (VAW), or if you have faith in real estate, you can invest in iShares US Real Estate ETF (IYR). Some good indices to follow are the S&P 500, the NASDAQ index, the Wilshire 5000, and the EAFE index.

What are the different types of index funds?

There's a lot of diversity when it comes to index funds and each fund has its own specific goals. Here are seven general types of index funds and the kinds of investments they make.

Broad market: invests in a wide variety of stocks; no defining characteristics for the stocks chosen; tries to capture as much of the market as possible

International: invests in international stocks; can be region-specific, sector-specific or just generally international

Sector: invests in specific sectors of the market like tech, real estate, retail, manufacturing, etc.

Dividend: invests in dividend producing stocks; can choose high yielding dividend or growth dividend stocks

Growth: invests in growth stocks and new companies

Equal Weight: invests equally in different sectors rather than based on their relative size in the stock market

Debt: invests in bonds; can have different strategies like stacking term lengths, certain yields, or bonds from certain sectors

What are some safe ways to invest in the stock market?
The safest way to invest in the stock market is to consistently invest long-term by letting your money sit and grow. Long-term investing decreases the effects of market risk, and investing consistently ensures your portfolio is always growing no matter what the market looks like. The best ways to invest are through ETFs or mutual funds that meet your long-term goals.

How can I tell how long a downturn will last?
A downturn, bear market, or recession usually lasts about a year on average. Bear markets affect short-term investments and trading but don't have much of an effect on long-term investments. Don't feel pressure to pull out your investments during a downturn; the market will turn around and you might regret that decision later. Some people actually invest more during bear markets to secure higher returns when the market turns, but it's okay to continue investing the same amount.

"You should be invested in the stock market as long as you're alive"

How much capital gains should I expect from my stocks?
There is no way to know exactly what your return will be, but there are some ways you can estimate. It's always good to look at the growth of a stock or fund over at least a seven to ten year period because ultimately long-term growth is what we're focusing on. Economic cycles usually repeat every ten years, so you can see how that investment performs during different cycles. You'll take the growth over that period and divide it by the number of years to get the average yearly growth. The S&P 500 has a long-term average yearly growth of 10.5%.

What are the downfalls of stocks?
Although there's a high likelihood of appreciation in the long run, there's no guarantee when it comes to investing in stocks. Also, the stock market is

in constant fluctuation, and this can play on the emotions of investors, especially inexperienced ones. The stock market has a lot of moving parts, and educating yourself on all the relevant information can take a lot of time.

Bonds

What is a bond?
A bond is a debt investment made by the bondholder to the bond issuer. When you invest in a bond, it's the same concept as taking out a loan, except you're the lender and the bond issuer is the borrower. When I buy government bonds, the government is borrowing from the Bank of Urenna Chimsomaga Okoye. Usually, they are issued by the government or corporations to raise capital. Bonds are called fixed-income investments because, unlike most other monetary investments, you are almost always guaranteed periodic income from the issuer until the end of the bond's life.

What is the par value?
The par value is the value at which a bond matures; it's the amount a bondholder will receive when they redeem the bond. A lot of bonds are sold at par, but some are issued at a discount (below par) or at a premium (above par).

What is a coupon rate?
The coupon rate of a bond is the interest rate of the bond, and it is a percentage of the par value. This determines how much income you receive periodically from holding the bond. They are normally fixed, but there are a few bonds that have variable coupon rates.

What is the maturity of a bond?
The maturity is the lifespan or expiration date of a bond. Unlike stocks, you can't hold a bond forever. At maturity, bonds are redeemed by bond

holders, and they receive the par value. Maturity dates can be anywhere from 4 weeks to 100 years after the issuance of a bond, but most long-term bonds are no longer than 30 years.

Why would I buy a bond at a premium?

Investors buy bonds at a premium if the interest rate on the bond is higher than the market yield. The bond "costs extra" because you're getting higher returns than you would from most other bonds. The interest is taken on the par value, so the return on your actual investment will be smaller than the coupon, but it may still be higher than the market rate. To know if it's worth the investment, use this formula:

$$\frac{par\ x\ coupon}{principal} > market\ rate$$

What's the difference between bonds and stocks?

Bonds	Stocks
Debt investments	Equity investments
Little to no appreciation potential	High appreciation potential
Guaranteed income	No income guarantee
Always redeemable	Highly redeemable but not guaranteed
Issued by the government and corporations	Issued by corporations
Little to no risk	Riskier

What are the shortest and longest bonds?

Bond maturities usually range from 4 weeks to 30 years, and different length bonds have different names:

Corporate Bonds

* *Commercial Papers:* maturity < 270 days
* *Bond:* 1 - 30 year maturity

Government Bonds

* *Treasury Bills (T-bills):* 4, 8, 13, 26, and 52 week maturities; pay no interest and are issued at a discount.
* *Treasury Notes:* 2, 3, 5, 7, and 10 year maturities
* *Treasury Bonds:* 10 - 30 year maturities

In building wealth, what are bonds good for?

Bonds, especially government bonds, are the safest, most sure way to earn passive income. Government bonds guarantee their interest payments and full repayment of the par value; if they don't have the money, they can just print it to make their payments. Bonds don't generally appreciate in value (only when bought at a discount), so they're not necessarily good for accumulation, but they're a great way to earn steady passive income.

What are some bond investment strategies?

Strategy	When It's Used
Bulleting: investing in bonds over time that all have the same maturity date	Normally used when the collective par value of the bonds will be used to make a purchase at a specific date shortly after the maturity date
Laddering: investing in bonds that each have a different maturity date	Normally used to take advantage of changing interest rates. If interest rates go up, you can reinvest the matured bonds to get a higher return. If rates go down, you would have already secured a higher rate.

Strategy	When It's Used
Barbelling: splitting investments between short-term and long-term bonds	Normally used to take advantage of changing interest rates and higher interest rates on long-term bonds. You're able to make more adjustments to interest rates with short-term bonds while securing the higher rate of long-term bonds.

Why don't I hear people talk about bonds a lot when it comes to money matters?

When it comes to investing and building wealth, bonds don't have a great impact. They provide a source of income but are not great for capital appreciation and therefore building wealth. It also takes large investments in bonds to receive reasonable amounts of income, and there are other ways to receive much more passive income for the same investment.

Do I need bonds as a young person?

It depends on what your financial goals are. If you're looking to build up your assets, avoid bonds and focus purely on stocks and real estate. If you're looking for ways to earn passive income, bonds provide that but require sizable investments for reasonable income. You can earn passive income with rental properties that give a higher rate of return, but you'd need more money to get a property than you would to get a bond. You can use short-term bonds if you're saving up for a purchase like a new car, a down payment on a house, or a vacation; I only recommend doing this if you have an idea of when you'll be making your purchase.

In what cases are bonds better investments than stocks?
Bonds are better investments than stocks when you're looking for more stable investments that aren't affected by market changes. Bonds are incorporated into moderate investment strategies to provide stability. They're also better if one of your investment goals is income because they provide guaranteed, consistent payments at a higher rate than most dividend stocks.

> *"Bonds, especially government bonds, are the safest, most sure way to earn passive income"*

Can I invest in bonds through the stock market?
Yes, you can do this by investing in bond ETFs. Just like any other ETF, the money you contribute is used to invest in various bonds or attempts to mimic bond indices. Bond ETFs tend to be stable in their value because bond values don't change once bought. They can fluctuate if current bond prices are changing and if new bonds are being bought by the fund.

I know bonds are a pretty safe and stable investment, but what are the risks?
Bonds are fixed-income investments that rarely appreciate in value. While they're great for stable passive income, they're terrible for wealth accumulation. Because they are so stable and steady, their real value decreases each year because of inflation, AKA purchasing power risk; the par value and interest payments don't adjust for inflation. Treasury Inflation Protection Securities (TIPS) are the only bonds that adjust for inflation; the coupon rate remains the same but the par value adjusts for inflation, which affects the value of interest payments. TIPS are usually sold at a lower interest rate than other bonds because they're adjustable. Another risk is that some bond issuers may default. These bonds tend to be high yield because they're riskier, just like people with a low credit score pay higher interest rates. The credit score equivalent of a bond is its

rating, which are provided by the S&P and Moody systems. The ratings go from D/C to AAA/Aaa, and ratings of BBB/Baa or higher are quality investments. Anything lower than that has a high risk of default and is often referred to as a junk bond.

How can I invest in bonds?

You can buy bonds from a broker, directly from the government, or through funds. With a broker — like Charles Schwabb, TD Ameritrade, or Fidelity — you would purchase the bond the same way you would purchase a stock from them. The same thing goes for investing in bonds through funds; it works the same way as stocks. Bonds may also be sold at a premium — or discount — when bought from a broker. For government bonds, you can buy them directly through treasurydirect.gov

Money Market

What is the money market?

The money market is the short-term bond market. Short term is usually classified as less than two years, but most money market instruments mature in less than six months. Depending on the instrument you use, you may or may not receive interest or be able to buy the bond at a discount.

What are different ways to invest in the money market?

The money market consists of T-Bills and short-term Treasury Notes, commercial papers, and Certificates of Deposit (CDs). CDs are bonds issued by banks that mature between three months and five years. You can get a CD with as little as $500. They are the only money market instrument that pays interest, usually semi-annually, but early withdrawal results in penalties.

How do you get a return from the money market?
Returns in the money market usually come from buying the bond at a discount. For CDs, interest rates are usually between .35% - .70% depending on the maturity, but some banks may offer rates as high as 3.5%.

Why would I invest in the money market?
The money market is best used as a short-term savings vehicle. I don't recommend using the money market for your safety net, but for all other savings, you may want to consider putting them in a money market instrument so you can earn something on that money.

Can I replace my savings with money market investments?
Replacing your savings with money market investments is a great idea for savings that are planned to be used at a specific date. Don't replace your safety net with money market investments; early withdrawal results in penalty charges, and you want that money to be completely liquid. If you're saving for a car, vacation, or a house, you may want to consider putting that money into a money market instrument or a short-term bond.

Retirement

Why is retirement planning important?
There are two main times in your life when you don't work: childhood and retirement. When you were a child, your parents were fully supporting you. However, when you retire, your parents won't be able to support you, and it's unlikely your kids will be able to fully support you, especially if they have kids of their own. Retirement planning allows you to prepare for that time in your life so you can support yourself without working. If you plan on retiring early, retirement planning is essential to achieving that goal. There will come a point when you won't be able to work anymore to sustain yourself, and having a plan for that period makes the transition a whole lot easier.

What should I be considering as I plan for retirement?

The point of retirement planning is to have enough income to sustain you through your retirement. But, what exactly is that income being used for? As always, your plan should include your vision for your life during that period. Would you want to travel? Would you want to move to another location? Would you want to be close to family? Would you like to be out and about or a homebody? One thing a lot of people don't consider is the medical expenses and physical limitations of getting older. One way people account for this is through Long-Term Care insurance, but another way to manage this reality is to develop a lifestyle of physical and mental care. Eat healthily, exercise regularly, and learn new things constantly. Sustaining yourself is not only being able to provide yourself with income but also being able to take care of yourself on your own.

How do I open a 401k?

401ks are provided by corporations as an employer-sponsored way to save for retirement. Depending on where you work and your position, you may or may not have access to a 401k specifically. Depending on the size of the company, the employer-sponsored retirement savings plan may be called something else: SEP IRA and SIMPLE for small businesses; 403b for non-profits; 457b for government organizations. If you are eligible for a plan, your employer will ask if you wish to participate; always say yes. Once you fill out the required documentation, your employer will handle the rest of the process to get your account set up.

If I don't have access to a 401k, can I still invest for my retirement?

Yes. If you want to save for retirement but don't have access to an employer-sponsored retirement plan, you can open an IRA (individual retirement account). They function very similarly to an employer-sponsored plan, except that your employer doesn't have to make contributions and you can only invest up to $6,000 a year, even if you open multiple accounts. You need income in order to open and contribute to an IRA. You can also just invest in the stock market directly, but you have to be disciplined enough to leave the money until you retire. Real estate is also a great way to invest for your retirement because, by the time you retire, your mortgages should be paid off, and all rents will be received as pure passive income.

What's the difference between a traditional and a Roth account?

A traditional retirement account is tax deductible on contributions, and a Roth account is tax free on withdrawals. For traditional accounts, the contributions are made with pre-tax dollars but withdrawals are taxed as income. With a Roth account, contributions are taxed but withdrawals are tax free. Roth accounts also have income restrictions; make sure you check the restrictions each year because they can change. For single people in 2022, if your AGI is less than $129k, you can make full contributions. For every $1,500 increase in AGI between $124k and $144k, your max contribution decreases by $600. For married people in 2022, if your AGI is less than $204k, you can make full contributions. For every $1,000 increase in AGI between $204k and $214k, your max contribution decreases by $600.

"The time you have until retirement is your best friend"

Can I have both a 401k and an IRA?

Yes. Many people who have both plans contribute to their 401k up to their employer's maximum match and then make further contributions to their IRA. IRAs tend to have a wider range of investment options and lower fees and having a Roth IRA gives you tax-deductible income in retirement. If you have a traditional IRA with any employer-sponsored plan, there are income restrictions on deducting your contributions; make sure you check the restrictions because they change each tax year. For single filers in 2022, contribution deductions phase out between gross incomes of $68k and

$78k. For married filers in 2022, contribution deductions phase out between gross incomes of $109k and $129k if you have the employer-sponsored plan and phase out between gross incomes of $204k and $214k if your spouse has an employer-sponsored plan.

How do I know if a Roth or traditional account is better for me?
This all depends on your expected retirement tax bracket and your current tax bracket. If you expect your retirement bracket to be higher than your current one, use a Roth account; if it's the reverse, use a traditional account. Either way, you'll be saving on taxes. If you're not sure, use a Roth account because it's likely your income will be higher in retirement because of long-term capital gains. You can also try to project your retirement earnings based on your contributions and your expected portfolio return. Also, remember that inflation changes the value of a dollar over time, so $150k will be worth significantly less when you're retiring and might be in a lower tax bracket than it's currently in.

Is it too early to start thinking about my retirement?
It's never too early to start thinking about retirement: in fact, the earlier the better. The main thing about retirement is having enough passive income to sustain you until you pass. Because of the magic of compound growth and time, the earlier you invest in your retirement — no matter how small — the more money you'll have to draw from in your retirement. You can open an IRA as soon as you start making income and, once you do, begin investing in it immediately.

Why should I start investing for my retirement now if I'm retiring in 30+ years?
Time makes all the difference when it comes to your investments growing. Let's say you're 30 and you're going to retire at 65. If you invest $100 a month into a fund that gives you 10% growth each year, you'll have about $340k available at retirement. If you wait until you're 35 to start, you will only

have $206k, but if you had started when you were 25, you could have had $555k. Five years of no contribution saves you $6,000 in the short run but costs you $215k in the long run; waiting another five years will cost you another $134k. There's no reason to put off investing in your retirement, no matter how young you are. The earlier you start — regardless of the size of your investment — the better off you will be. The time you have until retirement is your best friend.

Why should I contribute my 401k if it gives me less money in my take-home income?

From the perspective of someone who doesn't have a budget and who's not working towards a healthy financial life, contributing to your 401k wouldn't make any sense. However, as people who are taking control of their finances, contributing your 401k is one of the best ways you can invest. One, it's automatically taken out of your pay, so you don't get the opportunity to think about whether or not you want to spend or invest that money; that's one less thing for you to manually budget in your take-home income. If retirement contributions were already in your budget, your 401k makes that much easier. Two, a lot of employers match your contribution up to a certain amount, so you're actually doubling your contribution by contributing, giving compound growth more to work with.

"It's never too early to start thinking about retirement"

Can I use the money from my retirement account if I retire early?

You can, but you'll experience penalties for your withdrawal. Retirement distributions can officially begin at the age of 59½ but any taxable withdrawals before then are subject to a 10% penalty on top of tax obligations. There is a way to avoid the penalty with IRA withdrawals. If you take Substantially Equal Periodic Payment (SEPP), distributions based on your age and life expectancy, then you avoid the penalty. The withdrawal amount is calculated by dividing the account balance by your life expectancy factor. The downside of SEPP withdrawals is that, once you start the plan, you can't quit it and you can no longer make contributions to the account, so the growth of your account decreases with each withdrawal. If you're looking to retire fairly early, it's better to build up streams of passive income than to rely on your retirement accounts.

How much can I add to my retirement account each year?
You can only contribute $6,000 to your IRAs — if you have multiple, it's still $6,000 total — and employer-sponsored plans can have combined employee/employer contributions up to the lesser of your compensation or $56,000; SIMPLE plans have a contribution limit of $13,000. For IRAs, because the contribution is relatively significantly smaller, it's best to start as early as possible to take advantage of compound growth.

What exactly happens to my money when I contribute to my retirement account?
Your money is invested into different avenues, mainly the stock market and bonds. You are able to pick what kind of investment strategy you want, and the account managers will do the actual investing. Strategies are normally categorized as Conservative, Moderate, and Aggressive based on the stability and growth rate of the underlying investments and your risk tolerance. Most people are recommended to pick aggressive strategies until they're about 10 - 15 years out from retirement, which is when they'll switch to either moderate or conservative. You'll get quarterly and yearly statements from the broker so you can monitor the performance of your investments.

Real Estate

An Investment as Old as Time

At 20 years old, Amara moved out of her parents' house into an apartment close to her college campus. Her parents encouraged her to buy a condo instead of renting, but she didn't see what the difference would be. Eventually, she saved up enough to buy a condo at 23, even though she still didn't understand her parents' advice. She rented out a room to her friend and saw that she had $50 leftover each month after all the condo expenses were paid. The extra cash motivated her to buy more properties. Amara is now 29 with five properties that generate $700 of passive income for her every month.

At some point in your life, you're probably going to buy a house. Owning a house is one of the hallmarks of a healthy financial life. Have you ever thought about having multiple houses? Maybe for vacation or to escape the injustice that is winter. What about having a house, or five, that you don't live in? Providing homes to others and making money while doing so.

Most people recognize the importance of owning a home and recognize it as a rite of passage into adulthood. Owning land has always been a sign of prosperity and is now very accessible in our modern society. However, many people don't consider owning property when thinking about wealth, despite it being the oldest way to build wealth; if you owned land, you had a place to live and could grow crops and raise cattle for your survival and for commerce. Although our society has evolved, owning property still remains a staple in building wealth.

In this section, I want to expand your understanding of investments to include real estate. Real estate investing can feel more inaccessible than the stock market because of the quantity of cash required to buy properties. I will explain how you can get involved with real estate investing even if you have no money. Real estate, the oldest investment vehicle, will remain one of the best ways to build wealth and earn passive income.

What is real estate?
Real estate is property that consists of land and/or buildings. This includes houses, apartments, corporate buildings, farm land, restaurants, open fields and plots, etc.

Why is real estate one of the best ways to build wealth?
Real estate is the oldest way people have built wealth. The population is always growing, and we need space for people to live and for society to function. If you own space, you can rent it to someone to use and collect income. Over time, more and more space is needed, so the value of space goes up because there's a limited supply and a growing demand. This is why property values are always rising and why almost every wealthy person has some form of real estate.

What are different ways to invest in real estate?
Just like with stocks, there are short-term and long-term strategies for investing in real estate. However, there are also intermediary ways to get into real estate as well.

Birddogging/Driving for Dollars: looking for properties that are on the market or that look like they might be soon and providing the property information to an investor for a price; this saves the investor a lot of time in their investment process

Wholesaling: getting a property under contract and selling that contract to an investor; you find the property, do all of the analysis, put in an offer, and get it under contract all before you connect with an investor; all the investor has to do is close on the contract

Commercial: buying properties to rent out to individuals, families, or businesses; you can buy condos, houses, apartment buildings, retail buildings, corporate office buildings, etc.

Flipping: buying properties, mainly homes, and repairing them to increase the value and sell for a profit

REITs: Real Estate Investment Trusts (REITs) are essentially mutual funds for real estate; you invest in a REIT, along with many other investors, and the pooled money is used to buy many different properties; you own a portion of each property in the trust based

Land buying: buying a plot of land that can be rented out for various uses such as construction and agriculture

How can I invest in real estate with no money?
You can't actually invest in real estate with no money, but you can make money by getting involved in the investing process or getting a loan from a private investor to invest. The two main ways to get involved in the investing process with no money are birddogging and wholesaling. Birddogging is the easiest way to get involved in real estate because all you need to do is find properties on the market and give their information, and maybe an analysis, for a fee to an investor. With wholesaling, you need to find a distressed property, see if the owner is willing to sell, actually get the property under contract, and "sell" that contract to an investor.

Through these strategies, you'll learn a lot about property analysis and generate some cash that can later be used to purchase your own property.

To find a private investor, start with talking to older people around you; your network is your net worth. You can start with family and family friends since they already know you. Approach them with a proposal of your investment and your strategy to show that you've done the necessary work and that you're worth the investment. You could also join a local REIA (Real Estate Investment Association) and attend their events throughout the year. Most REAIs have an annual fee but some offer free attendance for certain events or for a limited time. In a REIA, you're connected to other investors in your area and are exposed to strategies, funding, connections, and possibly mentorship when it comes to real estate. Through a REIA, you could find investors to wholesale and bird dog for and some may be willing to lend you money to buy your first property. A REIA is a great resource for all current and potential real estate investors.

"Real estate is the oldest way people have built wealth"

How easy are birddogging and wholesaling?
Birddogging is as easy as knowing how to analyze a property and knowing a real estate investor. Most of property analysis is in the cap rate and the cost of potential repairs on the property. You can analyze the cap rate completely online, but you may want to visit properties to see what repairs they may need. Seven to ten hours out of the month — analysis and visiting properties — could get you a few hundred to a couple thousand dollars.

Wholesaling is more involved than birddogging but still doable. Most wholesalers look for distressed properties and try to convince the owners to sell. This will involve you driving around, analyzing the property, contacting owners, getting the property under contract, and then selling that contract to an investor who's interested in the property. While it is more involved, you make more money wholesaling, and within a few deals, you could have enough money to put a down payment on a mortgage.

What goes into managing a property, and is it a lot of work?

When you're managing a property, you're focusing on four main areas: getting tenants, collecting rent, paying expenses, and making repairs. The most time-consuming part is getting tenants into the property. You have to list the property, select and screen tenants, and have them sign lease agreements. The frequency of this process depends on the types of tenants you have and how likely they are to move. Collecting rent and paying expenses occurs on a monthly basis, so setting up reminders for yourself will be very useful. Repairs happen a few times out of the year, and you will usually call a contractor to do the repair for you.

What things should I look for when I'm looking to buy a property?

We buy properties for two reasons, investment or residence. For any investment, you need to first decide your investment strategy, mainly whether you're buying to flip or buying to rent. I suggest doing rentals because it's more passive, whereas flipping can practically be a full-time job. In any investment, the most important part is the expected return on that investment (ROI). Returns on rental properties are determined by how much you put down, the value of the property, and your net income. You want to pick properties in or close to areas of development; these areas will see an increase in property values and will have a good rental market. The main analysis you'll do is based on the capitalization rate, cap rate for short.

$$cap\ rate\ = \frac{NOI\ (net\ operating\ income)}{mortgage\ value}$$

$$= \frac{expected\ rental\ income - expenses\ excluding\ mortgage\ payment}{mortgage\ value}$$

You should only visit properties with a cap rate of 10%+. With a cap rate of 10%+, you'll have cash leftover after all expenses, including the mortgage, are paid. Properties with good cap rates for beginners tend to be townhomes that could use some cosmetic touch-ups like repainting or replacing appliances or flooring. These touch-ups will increase the property value and allow you to slightly increase the rent. As you continue investing, you can start looking for properties that need remodeling to increase their value and rental potential.

How do I determine rent on a property?

Rent is usually determined by the market, the features of your property, and the property value. Properties with larger square footage, more rooms and bathrooms, or that are closer to cities or areas of development tend to have higher rent. Yearly rent usually ranges between 10% - 13% of the property value, so 0.83% to 1.08% per month. You can see what rent is for properties with similar features to determine yours.

"You should only visit properties with a cap rate of 10%+"

How much of a down payment should I make?

The size of your down payment will be determined by how long you want to be paying off the mortgage and what else your money could be used for today. Usually down payments range from 10% - 20% or 5% for first-time homebuyers. Mortgages with higher down payments tend to have lower mortgage lengths. If you want to pay off the property early so you can receive all the rental income, you may want to make a larger down payment. If you want to have multiple properties, you may want to make a smaller down payment so you can buy other properties soon. A 13% - 16% down payment is a good range for both of these goals.

If you've saved up $30k for a property, you could put 20% down on a $150k property or put 13% down on two $115k properties. The $150k property will have lower mortgage payments and a lower mortgage length but the $115k properties will collectively rent for more and provide you with more net income.

96

What's a good mortgage interest rate?
Your interest rate will be determined by your credit score. For people with good credit, you should be looking for rates that do not exceed 5.5%. Interest rates also change with economic conditions and can range from 3% - 6% for high credit scores.

What's a buyer's market and a seller's market, and how can I identify them?
The real estate market is just like any other market in the economy and reacts to supply and demand. While there are times of high supply and others of high demand, you can't always predict how long those periods will last and when property values will level out. If you're looking to buy a property, don't try to predict the market. Look for the best deal given the current conditions of the market.

A buyer's market is when there are more houses on the market than there are people looking to buy them; supply is higher than demand. When this happens, property prices tend to drop to encourage buyers to buy. Buyers have the leverage in a buyer's market because they can negotiate the price down. Buyer's markets are usually marked by lower-than-average asking prices and longer-than-average times on the market. In a buyer's market, take your time to analyze multiple properties and negotiate the price down.

A seller's market, converse to a buyer's market, is when there are more buyers than there are people looking to sell their properties; demand is higher than supply. Property prices increase because buyers are competing for the property. Sellers have the leverage in a seller's market because they're likely to get more than the property is worth. Seller's markets are usually marked by higher-than-average bidding prices and shorter-than-average times on the market. In a seller's market, stick to your criteria but act fast when you find a property you like.

Should I invest in properties with other people?

Investing with other people is a great way to increase capital to purchase bigger properties that can generate bigger returns. When choosing investment partners, it's best to make sure you have the same investment goals and strategies and to discuss how ownership, responsibilities, and income will be divided. Make sure all agreements are in writing: you may even want to draw up a contract to formalize the partnership. It can be a fun experience to build wealth with friends and family, but make sure EVERYTHING is discussed and in writing before you start searching for properties.

What are the differences between using a property as an AirBnB versus as a rental property?

Rental	AirBnB
More stable income	Infrequent, periodic income
Charge per month	Charge per night
Daily charges lower	Daily charges can be higher
No furniture needed	Provide furniture
Tenants do their own cleaning	Frequent cleaning
Interact with tenants monthly and when repairs needed	Constant interaction with guests for booking and payments
Higher occupancy rate	Lower occupancy rate

What are all the expenses that come with owning a property?

You'll have to pay mortgage payments, homeowner's insurance, property taxes, HOA or condo fees, and maintenance/repairs. Utility payments are usually included in condo fees, and tenants usually pay their own utilities in homes. Every expense is paid on a monthly basis, except for maintenance and property taxes, which are paid on a quarterly, semiannual, or annual basis depending on the property location. If your mortgage has escrow, your insurance and tax payments will be paid monthly with your mortgage, and the lender will make the payments once a year. You may only have to make maintenance payments two to four times a year, but setting aside money for this expense each month will make paying for it easier when it comes up.

There are also upfront costs related to the purchase of a property, namely closing and reserves. Closing costs, ranging from 2% - 5% of the loan amount, can include the loan application fee, credit check fee, loan origination fee, inspection fee, appraisal fee, title insurance, title search fee, and transfer tax. Reserves are usually two months worth of mortgage payments so the lender can ensure you have the money to make your mortgage payments.

Can I buy properties in other states or even other countries?
You can, but you have to think about managing the property and the ownership laws in foreign countries. When buying properties in other states, the main things to think about are how you will visit the property to inspect it before you buy it, how you will show prospective tenants the place, and who you will call when repairs need to be made. The same applies for properties abroad, with extra considerations for the property laws of that country and the laws for ownership by non-citizens. It's a lot easier to manage properties within your own country, but you may consider another state for cheaper prices and good development.

What's a good-sized property to start off with as a new investor?
You can start off with a condo or a townhome. Townhomes may give you a higher return, especially since you can rent by the room, but condos are also good investments if the cap rate is high enough. The biggest difference between managing a house versus a townhome or a condo is

there's more maintenance to be done on a house because of the larger property size. As a beginner, you want to get used to managing tenants and paying expenses, so pick a property that'll allow you to have that experience without too many additional obligations.

Debt

Borrowing From Yourself and Others

Gozie is 28 and recently got married to Kemi, his girlfriend of five years. They both have student loans. Gozie had a car note and bought Kemi's ring with his credit card. They wanted to buy a home but knew that they'd have to buy their furniture on a payment plan. They were conflicted because they already had enough debt but felt that, as a married couple, they should have their own place. Kemi confided in her older sister about their dilemma, and she offered to have them stay with her family until they could afford everything that comes with the house. Although it wasn't ideal, they moved in with Kemi's sister for about a year. During that time, Gozie and Kemi paid off the ring and the car and were able to save enough money to buy their own house and all their furniture.

Having debt is as common as earning income. Almost everyone you know owes money to an institution for something they have, whether that be their house, their car, or the information that was crammed into their brain for four years to prove them worthy of employment. You can now buy so many things on a credit card or an installment plan. Whenever I get ads on Spotify, about half of them are trying to sell me contentment by way of a credit card. Debt is such an easy thing to acquire these days and is marketed as a tool to expand your options when, a lot of the time, it really restricts your future.

When we use debt to buy something, we see it as belonging to us. In reality, it only belongs to you as much as you've paid the lender back, and to make matters worse, you pay more than it's actually worth. You're not just borrowing from someone else to get the things you want; you're actually borrowing from your future to live in the present.

Not all debt is bad but most of the debt we get ourselves into is unnecessary and can be easily avoided. I want to give you context on when it's okay to have debt, how to manage your debt, and explain what credit is and what it's used for. For something that's as prevalent as the air we breathe, debt serves an important purpose in our lives. Therefore, it's important that we understand what it really is.

What is debt?
Debt is money that has been borrowed that is paid back incrementally with interest. It is the use of other people's money for purchases you don't currently have the money for. Interest is used more as a time payment for using the money the lender could've been using for other things.

Is it ever okay to have debt?
Yes, if that debt is being used for education or for real estate. Education and real estate, a home more specifically, are crucial aspects of life and are also both assets that contribute to building wealth. Going into debt to acquire these things is okay; you just need to make sure that the debt you get is manageable and reasonable for your income status.

Is there such a thing as good debt?
No and yes. Debt is never really a desirable thing to have because your money and the things you used that money to buy belong to someone else, whether wholly or in part. However, there are debts that are more

acceptable to have than others. Personally, the only debts I view as being acceptable are mortgages and student loans. With mortgages, you use them to buy your home or rental properties. You need somewhere to live and it's very unlikely you have hundreds of thousands of dollars lying around to buy a house in cash. Rental properties are assets, and they pay for themselves. Student loans help you get an education so that your professional value increases and you're able to earn at a higher income level; the income you receive as a result is what will pay off the loan. If your loans amount to more than 60% of your expected yearly income, I would say that's when it becomes bad debt.

What's the difference between a subsidized and an unsubsidized loan?
Most loans are unsubsidized in that interest accrues on the principal immediately. Subsidized loans tend to only be offered as student loans and interest doesn't accrue until after graduation, usually six months after graduation. The idea is that you shouldn't have to pay interest on a loan until you actually have the income to pay it, when you get a job.

"Buy cars in cash"

Should I pay more than the monthly minimum on my loan?
Yes, paying more than the monthly minimum will increase your credit score and decrease the amount of time spent paying the loan, resulting in you paying less overtime because you're paying less interest. How much over the monthly minimum should you pay? Once your savings, necessities, and investments are paid for, you can decide how much of your spending money you'd like to redirect towards your debt. You can be as aggressive or relaxed as you want, but if your life becomes miserable — not difficult but miserable — as a result, then you should redirect some of that back to yourself and your enjoyment.

Here's a practical example of paying above the minimum. If you have a balance of $1,000 with an interest rate of 18.%, it'll take you 9.5 years to pay off the balance, and you would've paid $925 in interest by making minimum payments of $25 a month. If you pay $10 extra each month, that's only $120 a year, and the time cuts to three years with interest payments of $315. You saved yourself six and a half years and $610 with only $10 extra each month.

Can I cancel my student loans? If so, how?
Federal student loans can be canceled or forgiven; however, private student loans cannot. Below is a list of circumstances that could make you eligible for loan forgiveness. For more information about how exactly to get your loans forgiven, visit
https://studentaid.gov/manage-loans/forgiveness-cancellation.

Public Service Loan Forgiveness: Ten years of repayment while working full-time for a government or non-profit organization

Teacher Loan Forgiveness: teaching full-time for five consecutive academic years in a low-income school; can forgive up to $17,500

Perkins Loan Cancellation and Discharge: certain employment and volunteer service

Total and Permanent Disability Discharge: becoming totally and permanently disabled

Borrower Defense to Repayment: if your school failed to do something regarding your loan or educational services related to the loan

False Certification Discharge: if your school falsely certified your eligibility to receive a loan

I graduated with a lot of student loans, and I don't want to be paying them off for the rest of my life. What strategies would you recommend for early repayment?
First, find ways to decrease all your other expenses and your miscellaneous purchases so you can reallocate that money to paying off

your loans. Remember to still pay yourself as you're paying others by having money, even if it's a little, budgeted for savings and investments. If the life you're living after reallocating your money is sustainable, continue aggressively paying off your loans. If it's not, adjust your budget so you can sustain your debt repayment strategy for at least two years. You will need a lot of discipline not to eat out, go on vacations, or buy too many clothes, but the freedom you'll experience after repayment will be more than worth it; and all that money you used for repayment will now be fully your money to invest in yourself and your future.

Should I pay off my student loans early if I can?

Yes. Early repayment of loans is always a good idea because you end up paying less interest and free up money earlier for your own personal use. How much extra you should pay is dependent on your budget. After you've determined your savings and investments and properly categorized your needs and wants, look at what wants you can cut back on long-term to contribute more to your repayment. This might mean eating more home-cooked meals, learning to do your own hair and nails, only having one streaming subscription, shopping at a local thrift store, and so many other practical ways to give you more cash.

Should I lease a car or buy one in cash?

Different people have different opinions on this, but my stand is that you should always buy a car in cash. You could use the argument that cars are a necessity just like a house. However, it's not the car that's the necessity but transportation, and unlike houses that increase in value over time, cars decrease in value the minute you drive them off the lot. If you leased a car, took it to Wendy's to get lunch, then returned to the same dealership an hour later and sold it back to them, you would receive less money than your lease amount and would still have some money left to pay on the lease. When you buy a car in cash, you acknowledge that it's a utility, and you also own the car outright. Yes, the car might be a bit older, but if it can get you from one place to another with no problems, then it's doing its job.

What is credit and why is it important?

Credit is a measure of how responsible you are when it comes to making payments on your financial obligations. It's used in the determination of interest rates on loans and whether or not a landlord will rent you their place; if your credit is bad enough, you can be denied loans. The only loans that don't look at credit are student loans and first-time credit cards. Because I believe in getting loans only for college and properties, I would say credit is important because it can determine if someone rents to you and your mortgage interest rate, which affects your monthly payment; a lower credit score means a higher interest rate which means a higher monthly payment. Landlords also need to trust that you can pay your rent on time because they have a mortgage to pay.

What is a FICO score?

A FICO score is a numerical valuation of your credit. All Americans who have had credit have a FICO score, and it's what's used in the determination of lending conditions.

Is a FICO score and a credit score the same thing?

Yes and no. FICO is one of many credit reporting companies, but it is also the most widely used among creditors. Although most people use these two interchangeably, your FICO score is only one way in which your credit can be measured.

What are the ranges for a credit score?

FICO scores range from 300 - 850, and subranges are often used to determine interest rates.

What things affect my credit score?
The chart below is a general breakdown of how your FICO score is determined. The five categories hold across the board, but the importance of each category can be more individual. For a first time borrower, payment history and amounts owed may be more heavily weighted, while for someone who borrows frequently, the length of their credit history and new credit might be more heavily weighted. In general, though, this is what goes into determining your credit score.

What's the difference between a credit and debit card?
A credit card allows you to use other people's money to make purchases, while a debit card is using your own money. When you use a credit card, you are incurring debt and will have to pay back what you use, sometimes with interest. Credit cards can help you build credit by showing your ability to pay back money you borrow.

How do credit cards work?
When you open up a credit card, look out for these things: the credit limit; the payment due date; the monthly minimum; the interest rate; the rewards policies. Remember that the purpose of a credit card is to build your credit, and each of these (except for the rewards) is a contributing factor.

The credit limit is the amount of money you have available to spend. It's advised not to use more than 25% of your limit at a time because that communicates to creditors that have a handle on your finances and are not in need of too much extra money for your everyday expenses.

The payment due date is when you need to pay at least the monthly minimum on your balance. When you're making your payments, pay more than the monthly minimum, usually between $20 - $40, and pay about a week before the due date; if you're able to, pay off the whole balance. This will communicate that you have the means available to make timely payments and will increase your credit score because you become more trustworthy.

When you pay off the balance in full before the due date, you don't incur any interest and only pay back what you initially paid for. Interest rates on credit cards are very high, 15% - 25%, and it's in your best interest to pay off the balance in full before the due date.

Rewards policies are only relevant for those who pay off their balances in full because then it's free money. Many credit cards offer cash back rewards for things such as groceries, gas, and retail, and some offer general cash back rewards. These rewards are a small percentage, usually 1% - 3%, of what you spent at these different places as an incentive to continue using the credit card. If you're paying 18% interest on your purchases but only receiving 1% cash back on them, you're still paying 17% interest and not really benefiting. To truly benefit from rewards, pay your balance off in full every month.

"A lower credit score means a higher interest rate which means a higher monthly payment"

What am I supposed to do with a credit card?

Credit cards are the best way to build credit without getting into real debt, and the best way to do this is by treating it as a debit card; your checking account balance becomes your new credit limit. Using your credit card as a debit card ensures that you only spend money that you have and are able to pay off the balance in full every month. The only way this works is if you are disciplined to make consistent payments on your card and not allow the balance to roll over to the next month. To be efficient, use your credit card just like you would use your debit card and don't make purchases you normally wouldn't make. An easy way to do this is by using it to pay for recurring purchases such as gas, your phone bill, groceries, or streaming services. The more consistent you are, the better your credit will be.

How can I improve my credit score?

Since your credit score is a numerical valuation of your ability to pay back money you've borrowed, you can improve your credit score by doing just that. If you have a low credit score, it probably means you have a history of not making timely debt payments or excessive use of debt.

1. Don't take out any more debt
2. Make consistent payments on the debt you have
3. Pay more than the monthly minimum

If you currently have no debt but have a low credit score, taking out a loan is still not an option because you will have a higher interest rate and monthly payments. If you're ready to become a homeowner, when you know you'll be making consistent monthly mortgage payments for 20 - 30 years, open a credit card and treat it as a debit card; *refer to the previous question*. If you know you're not responsible enough to be a homeowner, you can use rental payments to increase your score by having a rent-reporting service report your rental history to credit bureaus. Bottom line: credit is built, maintained, and improved by making consistent and timely payments for your financial obligations.

What are the advantages of a debit card?

Debit cards are great because you can only use the money you have to make purchases. You never run the risk of having to pay interest on your purchases, and you don't have to remember to make monthly payments. You make a purchase and your obligation ends there.

What are the advantages of a credit card?

Credit cards allow you the opportunity to build your credit without racking up real debt and offer cash back rewards. As mentioned earlier, the best way to maximize these advantages is to make consistent purchases and to pay off your balance in full before the due date each month.

"Use your credit card like a debit card and not like a gift card"

Are all credit cards the same?

There are store and service specific cards and then there are general credit cards which are issued by banks. Each bank has its own credit policies, but in general, things are consistent across the board when it comes to making payments and the things you can use your card for. Most differences are in their cash-back policies, which is not the primary reason for getting a credit card.

How is interest determined on my credit card?

Your interest rate is determined by your credit score first and foremost. If you don't have a credit score, your interest rate will be determined based on where you open your card and can range anywhere from 15% to 25%. People with good credit usually have an interest rate of 13% - 14%. Interest only accrues if your balance rolls over to the next month. The interest you pay month to month is the interest rate divided by 12 on the balance of your account. If you have a $100 balance and an 18% interest rate, your interest payment for the month will be $1.50. Each month, interest applies not only on the balance but also on the accrued interest; this is called compound interest. Continuing with the example, if you only pay your monthly minimum of $30 next month, interest will be calculated on $71.50 instead of $70. These numbers are low because I started with a low balance, but with higher balances and more time, the interest payments really start to add up.

Aren't credit cards good for emergencies?

Credit cards are only good in emergencies when you've depleted your emergency fund and all your other savings. Emergencies and unexpected situations are a normal part of life and should be factored into your finances by means of a budgeted emergency fund. If after all your considerations and planning, your emergency fund and savings are insufficient, using a credit card is understandable.

Should I get another credit card?

My advice is no, but there are some people who are able to handle multiple cards. I personally don't think you need more than one credit card. You're already having to manage your original card by keeping up with payments and adding another card onto that is another thing to worry about. Stick to make consistent, full balance payments on your one card, and your credit score will do just fine. If you feel like you can handle making payments on multiple cards and be disciplined enough to treat them both like debit cards, getting another card won't hurt you. Having multiple lines of credit communicates to credit reporters that you're able to handle multiple loans and can potentially increase your credit score.

Taxes

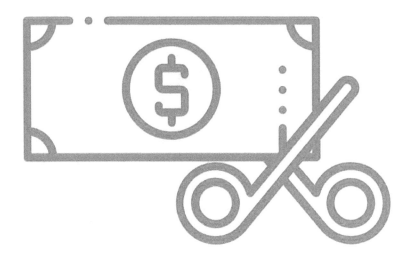

Uncle Sam's Cut

In college, Chidi came across financial literacy as he was researching ways he could earn some extra money. He's been really consistent with his budget and investing and made sure to buy his first car in cash. When he turned 27, he started trading and investing in real estate; he decided to buy properties under an LLC. He had some high returns his first year of trading and was making about $150 a month from his rental property. He decided to see an accountant for that tax year. The accountant said if he buys properties under an S-Corp rather than an LLC, he could save on his taxes and suggested that if he plans to continue real estate investing and trading, he should develop a long-term relationship with a CPA. Now, at 30, Chidi meets with his CPA throughout the year to discuss tax strategies for his investments.

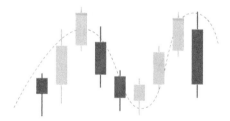

When I hear the word taxes, my mind goes to the color gray, a feeling of stress and sadness, a stack of papers, and the IRS breathing down my neck. Taxes are not the most fun thing to talk about, but we can't escape them. They are just another expense we have to pay, except that we can't elect to not have this expense. I need water to shower but at least I can make the choice to shower this month. I can't just not pay my taxes; I don't even get the chance to make that decision most of the time. What kind of "free" country is this?

All jokes aside, taxes can be a very confusing part of our finances because we're never taught how to handle them but are expected to file them yearly. One accident when filing could cost you thousands of dollars. There are A LOT of tax documents, and it can be overwhelming to figure out what's really relevant to you and your money. Tax situations and considerations also change as you accumulate wealth, and it's important to be aware of these changes even before you start your wealth journey.

This section explains the basics of taxes and what you need to know in order to properly file your return. The information provided is meant to make taxes less daunting by educating you on all the ways you may be required to pay taxes and even what documents you'll need to file them. Hopefully I can add a tint of blue to that gray and make the IRS's breath a little less hot.

What are taxes?
Taxes are money collected for government spending through taxpayer's income, transactions, and assets. You can expect to be taxed if you receive money, buy something, or own real estate. Most of the taxes people pay are on their earned income.

What are the different types of taxes?
There are taxes at the local or municipal level, the state level, and the federal level. Each level collects specific types of taxes:

Local Taxes
- *Property taxes* - taxes on certain property items i.e. real estate

State Taxes*
- ❖ *Sales taxes* - taxes on the exchange of goods and services
- ❖ *Income taxes* - taxes based on earned income
- ❖ *Capital Gains taxes* - taxes on the realized appreciation of assets

Federal Taxes
- ❖ *Income tax* - taxes based on earned income
- ❖ *Payroll tax* - taxes on income that contribute to one's personal social welfare i.e. Social Security and Medicaid
- ❖ *Capital Gains taxes* - taxes on the realized appreciation of assets
- ❖ *Corporate tax* - taxes based on business income
- ❖ *Estate tax* - taxes on the execution of an estate (transfer of assets)

the presence of these taxes vary from state to state

What's the purpose of taxes?
Taxes exist to establish and maintain the infrastructure and welfare of our society. The government uses tax money to build roads, develop schools, provide grants, set up social welfare programs, fund the military, and provide a number of other services to keep our society running.

What are the tax rates for each category?

Category	Tax Rate
Property Tax*	average of 1.1%
Sales Tax*	0% - 9.55%
Income Tax State*	0% - 5.8% for lowest tax bracket 0% - 13.3% for highest tax bracket
Federal	10% - 37% depending on tax bracket

Category	Tax Rate
Capital Gains Tax *State**	0% - 13.3%
Federal	
- Short-term - Long-term	*factored into income tax* 0%, 15%, 20% depending on size of gains
Payroll Tax	6.2% social security 1.45% medicare
Corporate Tax	21%
Estate Tax	18% - 40% depending on size of estate

*State tax rates vary from state to state

How do taxes work?

Taxes are taken from the income you receive to help fund government spending. There are different tax rates for different types of income at the federal level, and every state has their own rates as well. Income and payroll taxes are taken automatically from your gross income. Every year when you file a tax return, you're letting the government know how much income you really made that year, within and outside of your job, and how much of it is no longer in your hands due to various expenses; the resulting number is your taxable income. Your taxes are then calculated from your taxable income and measured against the taxes that were already taken; you get a refund if you overpaid or pay the balance if you underpaid. Taxes are also taken as a percentage of property you own at the local level.

What is the difference between gross income, net income, AGI, and taxable income?

Gross income is the income that you receive throughout the year from your job, investments, or wealth transfers before any taxes are taken. Net income is the take-home income that you receive after taxes are taken, along with any other wealth transfers. Your AGI, or adjusted gross income, is your income after adjustments and deductions are applied. Taxable income is the layman's term for AGI, and it's the income on which your taxes are calculated.

"You need to know all the ways in which you've received income and all the ways you qualify for adjustments, deductions, and credits"

What is a deduction?

Deductions are expenses that are removed from your gross income to better represent any untaxed money you have. If you've used $1000 this year to buy gas, you've already paid sales tax on that money when it was transferred to the tax station, so there's no need for you to pay tax on it again because you no longer have it.

There are standard and itemized deductions. Standard deductions are set amounts people can use to reduce their taxable income depending on their filing status. Itemized deductions are a list of deductible expenses outlined by the IRS. With itemized deductions you need to have a record of said expenses to be included. Everyone is allowed a deduction, and it's advised to pick the deduction that will result in a lower taxable income. Most people choose standardized because it's easier to file.

What are adjustments?

Adjustments, similar to itemized deductions, are a list of pre-determined expenses that can be subtracted from your gross income; the resulting number is your AGI. Unlike deductions, only those who have proof of said expenses are able to file them. Some things on the list include educational expenses, medical expenses, retirement contributions, and legal obligations.

What are credits?

Tax credits are incentivised tax "discounts"; they reduce the taxes you pay as a reward for things that benefit society. Tax credits directly reduce the final tax obligation, whereas adjustments and deductions indirectly reduce tax obligation by reducing taxable income. Credits are given for having a family, using sustainable energy, making retirement contributions, going to college, having health insurance, and a few other things.

What are tax brackets?

Tax brackets are the division of taxable income levels and their corresponding tax rates. These only exist for income tax; every other tax has their own tax rates. In America, because we have a progressive tax system, tax rates increase with higher income. Income tax is calculated marginally and not on your entire income. If you file as a single and have an AGI of $50,000, the first $10,275 is taxed at 10%, the next $31,500 (up to $41,775) is taxed at 12%, and the remaining is taxed at 22%. Tax brackets change from time to time so make sure to know what your bracket is for the upcoming tax year. Here are the tax brackets from the 2021 tax year.

Tax Rate	Single	Head of Household	Married Filing Jointly	Married Filing Separately
10%	$0 - $10,275	$0 - $14,650	$0 - $20,550	$0 - $10,275
12%	$10,276 - $41,775	$14,651 - $55,900	$20,551 - $83,550	$10,276 - $41,775
22%	$41,776 - $89,075	$55,901 - $89,050	$83,551 - $178,150	$41,776 - $89,075

Tax Rate	Single	Head of Household	Married Filing Jointly	Married Filing Separately
24%	$89,076 - $170,050	$89,051 - $170,050	$178,151 - $340,100	$89,076 - $170,050
32%	$170,051 - $215,950	$170,050 - $215,950	$340,101 - $431,900	$170,051 - $215,950
35%	$215,951 - $539,900	$215,951 - $539,900	$431,901 - $647,850	$215,951 - $323,925
37%	$539,901+	$539,901+	$647,851+	$323,926+

What are all the ways the government takes our money before we get our paycheck, and where do each of them go?

You can actually check this on your W-2. Before your direct deposit hits your account, the government takes out money for social security, medicare, and income tax at all levels. Social security pays income to retired people and disabled people; your social security contributions also affect how much you'll receive in retirement or in the case you become disabled and can't work. Medicare is health care for those who receive social security. Sometimes, the wages and tips on your W-2 for each category may differ, and this is because certain things can be taken out of your pay that are exempt from federal income tax but not exempt from social security or medicare payments.

What exactly is being taxed?

Taxes are taken on basically all documented transfers of money within a society. You pay taxes on goods and services, earned income, realized capital gains, inheritance, and large sum monetary gifts. Corporations pay taxes on their profits and the money they pay their employees. Taxes are also taken on property at the state and local levels. You don't pay taxes when you give your friend $50, but whatever they choose to spend that money on is taxed.

Do I need to file a tax return?

If you make over a certain amount of income, you need to file a tax return to ensure you've paid all your taxes. For single people, the income limit is $12,550, and for married people filing jointly, the limit is $25,100. Even if your income is below the limit, you still want to file a return because there's a high possibility that you'll get a refund.

What information do I need to know to file my taxes?

You need to know all the ways in which you've received income and all the ways you qualify for adjustments, deductions, and credits. For income, you'll need your W-2 if you're an employee, Schedule SE for self-employment, Schedule K-1 for business partnerships, and 1099s for all other income. For adjustments and deductions, the organizations where you made the payment will provide a tax document for you to file.

How do I file my taxes?

There are many free online tax filing services that allow you to file your own taxes, including the IRS; some of the platforms may require you to have an account with them. You'll need to gather your income documents and any documents you can use for deductions and adjustments. Once you have all your information, input your data into the relevant tax forms in the system. Once everything is imputed, submit the form, and the system will send your return to the IRS. If you receive income outside of a W-2 or are eligible for credits, you may not be able to file your taxes for free, but you can still self-file online for a fee. You can also pay a tax accountant to file for you.

Should I have a tax accountant?

Tax accountants are good to have when you have a complicated financial life. If you only receive income from your job and don't have many assets, you don't necessarily need an accountant. If you have multiple streams of income, are a business owner or self-employed, or have large cash-flowing assets, you should consider getting a tax accountant. Tax accountants not only help you to accurately file your taxes but can also help you strategize to reduce the amount of taxes you pay in a given year. You also have to consider the time versus cost investment: if you hire an accountant, will the cost of paying them be worth the time you save if you file your own return? Not everyone needs a tax accountant: not having one should not prevent you from having a tax plan.

"Everyone should pay their fair amount of taxes: not more, not less"

How can I create a tax plan without an accountant?

Tax planning focuses on reducing your tax liability by making contributions and by claiming all applicable deductions and credits. A great and very easy tax plan is to contribute any extra money at the end of each month or at the end of the year to your retirement accounts. You can even revise your budget so you intentionally make more contributions to retirement accounts throughout the year. When you contribute to your accounts, you not only save on your taxes, but you're directly redirecting that money from the government to yourself.

For deductions, keep records of anything that could be itemized. If your itemized deduction value is greater than the standard, itemize. Also, make sure you're claiming all credits you're eligible for.

Your tax planning deadline is December 31st of each year, so make sure all your contributions are done by then so they can be factored into your tax return.

What happens if I don't file my return in time?

You can file your return after the April 15th deadline up until October 15th, the extension deadline, but you'll have to pay a 5% Failure to File penalty on your unpaid taxes for each month you don't pay your taxes. If you owe nothing, you pay nothing, but you won't get a refund either if you're due one. You can wait three years max to file for unclaimed refunds.

When do I need to file my taxes?

The deadline to file taxes and pay your taxes is April 15th. If April 15th falls on a weekend, then the deadline is the next business day. During certain economic circumstances, like COVID, the deadline may be extended. If you're not able to pay by April 15th, you can file for an extension for which the deadline is October 15th.

How early can I file my taxes?

Tax filing for each year opens between January 15th and February 1st, when taxpayers are expected to receive their final pay stub from the previous year. You can pay your taxes anytime between then and April 15th.

What happens if I pay too much or too little in taxes?

If you end up paying too much in taxes, you'll receive a refund check for the overpayment. If you end up not paying enough, you'll have to pay the balance of your taxes.

How is it possible that I might pay too much or too little in taxes if it's taken out of every paycheck I get?

The only taxes that are taken out of your paycheck are employee income taxes, medicare taxes, and social security taxes. As listed earlier, there are other taxes you may need to pay depending on what kinds of wealth transfers you received in the previous year. Also, taxes taken out of your paycheck don't reflect the deductions and credits you're eligible for.

How do I pay my taxes?

You can pay your taxes through electronic withdrawal, direct pay from your bank account, or by card or cash. The most convenient way to pay is with electronic withdrawal or card payment through your e-filed return; you provide your account or card information with your return, and the IRS takes the money out of your account. With direct pay, you'll also pay using your account information, except through the IRS website instead of through your return. For card payments, you can pay online or over the phone for a fee. For cash payments, you need to sign up for a cash payment through ACI Payments and make your payment through one of their listed retail stores.

For more detailed information about how to pay your taxes, visit https://www.irs.gov/newsroom/how-to-pay-your-taxes

Is trying to reduce the amount of taxes you pay unethical? Isn't that just tax evasion?

No, there are legal and incentivized ways to reduce your taxes, and everyone should pay just their fair amount of taxes: not more, not less. Most times, when people find ways to reduce their taxes, they have to tie their money up into some kind of investment and not use it to claim deductions. Tax evasion happens when you illegally file your taxes by falsely reporting income, deductions, and credits.

Go Start Your Design

The last story I want to tell is the story of you. You came to this book with questions, confusion, doubt, curiosity, and ambition. You knew your finances are important and decided to equip yourself to take control of your life. You were looking for answers, guidance, and clarification and are leaving not only with knowledge but also confidence. You know the areas of your financial life that need work and you know what to do to improve them. With the information you've received, you change the trajectory of your life and encourage those around you to do the same, providing them with knowledge to inspire confidence to go after the things they desire.

Money exists to help us live the lives we dream of. In order to extract that function, we need to understand how money operates. By reading this book, you've gained the understanding you need to employ your money and construct your life. As you progress on your financial journey, remember to enjoy the process and continue to live your life along the way. Money will help you to live your dream life in the future, but it also allows you to live your life now.

I want to close this book by tying everything back to the Financial Tree of Life. All this new information may be a bit overwhelming and I want to provide some practical steps you can start doing immediately. As mentioned in the "Mindset" section, the most important parts of your financial life are the roots of the Financial Tree of Life: financial literacy; goals and vision; mindset and habits; income and budget; network and circle. All my advice is centered around developing these roots so your tree can flourish.

1. Create a vision for your life and set measurable goals around that vision
2. Create and stick to a budget that reflects where you are now and what your vision is
3. Talk to the people around you, meet new people, and educate others
4. Invest $100 (or as much as you're able to) into the VOO index fund NOW
5. Work towards paying off all your debt outside of your mortgage
6. Reflect on your mindsets and preconceptions about money
7. Keep reading and educating yourself

I hope this book has given you the knowledge and confidence you need to design your dream life.

Glossary

401k Plan: a corporate-sponsored retirement plan

403b Plan: a non-profit-sponsored retirement plan

457b Plan: a government-sponsored retirement plan

Adjustment: a list of pre-determined expenses used to reduce gross income

Aggressive Investing: a strategy that prioritizes growth and has higher risk

AGI (Adjusted Gross Income): income after tax adjustments and deductions are applied

Asset: property that someone owns that has a lot of monetary value and/or has the potential to increase in value

Asset Class: a group of investments that have similar characteristics

Barbelling: splitting investments between short-term and long-term bonds

Barter: the exchange of one good for another

Birddogging: looking for properties that are on the market and providing the property information to an investor for a price

Bond: a debt investment made by the bondholder to the bond issuer

Budget: a plan of how to spend your money

Bulleting: investing in bonds over time that all have the same maturity date

Call Option: the ability to buy 100 shares of a stock at a given price if the stock's price goes up before the option's expiration date

Capital Gains Tax: taxes on the realized appreciation of assets

Capitalization Rate: a rate — based on rental value, expenses, and market value — used to determine if a property is a good investment;

(Rent - Expenses) ÷ Market Value

Commercial Real Estate: real estate rented out to individuals, families, or businesses

Common Stock: stock that has voting rights and the ability to appreciate in value

Compound Growth: the exponential growth of an investment

Conservative Investing: a strategy that prioritizes stability and has lower risk

Corporate Tax: taxes based on business income

Coupon Rate: the interest rate of the bond

Covered Call: selling a call option

Credit: a measure of how responsible someone is when it comes to making payments on your financial obligations

Credit Score: a numerical valuation of your credit

Cryptocurrency: a decentralized, digital currency

Debt: money that has been borrowed that is paid back incrementally with interest

Deduction: expenses that are removed from gross income

Diversification: the allocation of your investments in multiple different asset classes to reduce the effect of risk from any one asset

Dividend: a distribution of a company's profit to its shareholders

Dollar-Cost Averaging: investing the same amount of money consistently

Entrepreneurship: setting up a business in the hope of profit

Envelope Method: a budgeting method that uses multiple accounts, or envelopes, with set amounts of money for each category

Estate Tax: taxes on the execution of an estate (transfer of assets)

Equity: the value of your ownership in an asset; can be lower than market value

Financial Literacy: having the knowledge about how money operates

Financial Freedom: the state where your assets are producing enough passive income to replace your earned income

Flipping: buying properties and repairing them to increase the value and sell for a profit

Gross Income: the income that is received throughout the year from a job, investments, or wealth transfers before taxes are taken

Growth Stock: stock of companies whose main objective is growth

Income: any money you receive through work, investments, as a gift, or by inheritance

Income Stock: stock that issues dividends to their stockholders

Income Stream: a way in which you earn income (i.e. a job, a business, investments)

Income Tax: taxes based on earned income

Index Fund: a fund designed to mimic or perform better than an underlying index

Investment: the placement of money into a potential asset in hopes of increased value

Investment Fund: a pool of money used to make investments for multiple contributors

Laddering: investing in bonds that each have a different maturity date

Liability: property or cash on which the value is paid to a lender with interest

Market Capitalization: the dollar value of all of a company's shares

Market Value: the value at which an asset can be sold

Maturity: the lifespan or expiration date of a bond

Moderate Investing: a strategy that combines aggressive and conversative strategies, aiming for growth without too much risk

Money Market: the short-term bond market

Mutual Fund: an actively managed and traded investment fund

Net Income: the take-home income after income and payroll taxes are deducted from the gross income, along with any other wealth transfers

Net Worth: the value of your assets minus the balance of your liabilities

Par Value: the value at which a bond matures

Passive Income: money that is earned with little to no effort compared to a traditional job

Payroll Tax: taxes on income that contribute to one's personal social welfare

Percentage Budgeting: a budgeting method that allocates percentages to different outlined categories.

Preferred Stock: stock that has priority claims over common stock, issues dividends, but usually has no voting rights or appreciation potential

Principal: the contributions to an investment

Risk: the possibility of financial loss

Rule of 72: a quick analysis trick used to determine the performance of an investment over time;

$72 \div$ the growth rate = # of years for investment value to double

Sales Tax: taxes on the exchange of goods and services

Simple Growth: the constant increase in the value of the principal

Speculation: investments with significant risk that advertise significant returns

Stock: a certificate of partial ownership within a public company

Stock Broker: a person or a company that is licensed to execute stock trades for investors

Stock Index: a measure of the performance of the stock market, or a subset of the market, by tracking the performance of selected stocks meant to represent that market

Tax Bracket: the division of taxable income levels and their corresponding tax rates

Taxes: money collected for government spending through taxpayer's income, transactions, and assets

Value Stock: stock that appears to be underpriced based on the strength of the company's books (their assets)

Wealth: the possession of an abundance of valuable assets that can converted into cash

Zero-Based: a budgeting method where every dollar is "spent" — or accounted for — at the end of each month

Made in the USA
Monee, IL
09 April 2023